When it came time to develop the theme for the 1995 Variety Club "Show of Hearts" Telethon, we didn't have to look any further than Peter Legge's newest book, *You Can If You Believe You Can*, for inspiration.

This memorable collection of stories and anecdotes speaks to so many of the wonderful qualities we see in the mentally and physically challenged children served by Variety Club. Faced with daunting obstacles, they live life with true courage, determination, optimism and joy.

A host of the annual Telethon for almost 20 years, Peter has been touched by the indomitable spirit of our special kids, a spirit you'll find captured here between these pages.

Please accept this book as a token of our thanks for your generous contribution to the 1995 Show of Hearts. I hope you find these stories help reaffirm your belief in your own dreams.

Barry Law, Chairman
1995 Variety Club Show of Hearts Telethon
Variety Club of B.C.

YOU CAN IF YOU BELIEVE YOU CAN

Peter Legge
with
Duncan Holmes

EAGLET PUBLISHING

Eaglet Publishing
401, 4180 Lougheed Highway
Burnaby, British Columbia, V5C 6A7 Canada

Canadian Cataloguing in Publication Data

Legge, Peter, 1942-
    You can, if you believe you can

Includes index.
ISBN 1-55056-289-4

   1. Success.   2. Self-actualization (Psychology).
I. Holmes, Duncan.   II. You Can If You BelieveYou Can
BF637.S8L44 1994   158'.1   C94-910-229-6

First Printing   July 1994
Second Printing   December 1994
Third Printing   October 1995

Jacket design by Gavin Orpen
Typeset by Sheila Lloyd and Ina Bowerbank
Edited by Sheila Jones of International Wordsmiths Ltd.
Printed and bound in Canada by Friesen Printers

*Dedicated to all those who
believe they can —
and who have made
the commitment to begin.*

Other Books by the Author

How to Soar With the Eagles

CONTENTS

ACKNOWLEDGEMENTS

I never thought I would publish a first book, let alone a second. But in my line of work, the stories keep coming and if the feedback from How to Soar With the Eagles is any indication, many benefit from their telling. Inspiration for a book of this kind comes from a variety of sources — the words and achievements of others, the old and new parables of the ages, the ordinary and not so ordinary happenings in my personal and business life. Who to acknowledge? The medical team and the support staff who pulled me through a brush with cancer. Without them, there would have been no second book. Again, my supportive family, my wife Kay and my three beautiful daughters Samantha, Rebecca and Amanda, my mother and father Win and Bernie Legge — every member continues to inspire me. And my friend Duncan Holmes, who was my editor and mentor for How to Soar With the Eagles; Duncan did it again with this book after too few lunches and a minimal number of meetings. His magic touch is remarkable. I thank Karen Foss and Neil Soper, my Executive Vice Presidents of Canada Wide Magazines, for their continuing support of my eclectic lifestyle. I thank my assistant Janice Maxwell, who helps keep my life in order, and Corinne Smith, Gavin Orpen, Sheila Lloyd, Ina Bowerbank and Robin Roberts, who also made unique contributions. Lastly and again collectively, I acknowledge those whose stories we have included. They are the ones who inspired this second publishing visit.

Peter Legge
Vancouver, B.C.

It may be

those who do most,

dream most.

— **Stephen Leacock**
   Canadian Humorist

INTRODUCTION

A BOOK IS NOTHING MORE than words and paper, but surely there are few things more powerful than books. Books have changed the lives of individuals and there is no doubt at all that they have changed the world.

From Plato's Republic to whatever title that is tops on today's list, books have made their mark on an evolving world. We read them, we are motivated and moved by them, they make us laugh, make us cry, they teach us, and they make us think.

You might think that with all of the wonderful stuff that's available in books, we would all be continuously reading.

Not so. In Canada, and most likely anywhere else, 93 per cent of the books purchased today are purchased by just one per cent of the population.

Another statistic that might amaze you? Ninety per cent of the population doesn't read a book all year!

Too busy? Maybe. But doing what? Watching television? More mind-numbing pap that does little more than fill time? Working to save money to buy one more VCR, one more TV?

Of course, we are overloaded with information. As a publisher of a number of national and regional magazines, I know that I'm one of the worst offenders. Our biggest seller is TV Week Magazine that does little more than list what's on television!

Technology has made it very easy to pinpoint messages directly to the groups of people we think might be interested in those messages.

Check the magazine stands at your local supermarket. If you ride a mountain bike, there's a magazine just for you. If you want to develop your bust or reshape your backside, there are magazines just for you. There are magazines for greenhouse growers, rock climbers and on and on.

So if we have ten marginal interests and we buy ten magazines, just *browsing* through them all can take up a ton of reading time. The long articles must wait for tomorrow, but tomorrow there's another magazine. And so on. Have you ever received or bought a magazine and never read it? Bet you have!

So what about books? The Great Books, the books that can motivate our lives? The books and the messages within them that can lead us onto higher roads, lift us out of sloughs of despair, inspire us, teach us, change our lives? Where do *books* fit in?

E.D. Hirsch Jr. wrote a great book called Cultural Literacy in which he argues that children in the United States are being deprived of the basic knowledge that enables them to function in contemporary society. He says they lack cultural literacy, a grasp of the background information that writers and speakers assume their audiences already have.

That makes me very nervous. With nobody reading anything much, with a generation of cultural illiterates on their way to adulthood, how guarded must I be in making a presentation? Do I talk from *my* frame of reference, which admittedly isn't too literate anyway, or do I presume that everything must be in — for want of a better term — TV Speak? Hopefully, there is a middle ground, where I can inspire without insulting, where I can do what I do without intimidating.

I don't pretend to be any kind of cultural genius. My words and lessons were learned in life, not in universities. But I have done some reading. Earl Nightingale, who has always been an inspirational hero, passed on some good lessons that have helped me immensely in the way I have done things. If you want to accelerate your career, he said, learn to be a public speaker. With some experience in comedy and stage work, I took his advice and it has worked beyond all expectations.

If you want to add depth to the speaking you do, others told me, publish a book. So I did that too. Stories I have told on the podium became chapters for a book I funded and published called How to Soar With the Eagles.

It was never intended to be more than a 'take home' from a Legge presentation, a book of personal stuff that might end up in the bathroom library, a quick read on a rainy Sunday.

I was amazed at the reaction. It became a Canadian bestseller, it went into a third printing. It brought me phone calls and letters of appreciation and it doubled my speaking engagements. It influenced the way I spoke, made me more anecdotal, drew out more of *me*.

It was something I sent when I wanted to say thank-you. It was a gift when I knew that a chapter within it might help someone in difficulty get back on track. It was an enterprise that was enormously satisfying.

There are always more stories and that's why there is a second book — as simple, as imperfect, as honest as the first.

Most of the chapters are short because I know you don't have a lot of time. Read one now and another six months from now. It doesn't matter. I won't make you culturally literate, that will have to come from the wisdom of others. All I have done in this book is to pass on a bit of my life because I believe it's a life worth sharing.

Thank you for joining me on another flight. Thank you for saying I can, because I believe I can.

Peter Legge
Vancouver, B.C. Canada, July, 1994

CHAPTER 1

"Pete, You Have Cancer!"

IN THE FALL OF 1992, I was driving back to my office from an important lunch in downtown Vancouver when the phone rang in the car. I've had a phone in the car for quite a while, but it still amazes me that you can actually BE called and MAKE calls from a CAR!

It was my doctor.

"Pete," he said. "I don't know what you're doing right now, but you need to come to my office immediately."

"What's the matter?"

"You have cancer."

On a CAR phone!

I pulled off to the side of the road and began to cry. Rolling tears. And between the tears, my life, every important moment I had ever lived, rolled too, like a great screen before me. Cancer! The terrifying words I had just heard triggered all kinds of levers and emotions that most of the time were inactively just THERE. Now, like circuit breakers snapping into life at a hydro sub-station, they were part of terrifying real time.

Without doubt, I was going to die. Done. Finished. And with approaching death, my value system, my roots, my life's foundations were about to be tested as never before. My proclaimed faith was right on the line.

But we humans come around. The survival instinct cuts in. Severely beaten, but already feeling hints of reserve strength, I immediately wondered if I could perhaps overcome whatever it was I now had. Could I be as positive as I tell people in speeches and seminars around the world that I really am? Could I impact my OWN life as I've been told I impact the lives of OTHERS?

When I called him back, my doctor told me to pick up my wife and come to his office. Kay was home from her studies and the two of us went hand in hand to see my doctor.

"A simple operation," he said in his best airline pilot voice. "Six to eight stitches and about twenty minutes. We're going to take a piece from your butt and use it to patch your face." Interesting. My backside suddenly felt exposed!

They took me into the hospital, laid me down and covered my face. It wasn't THAT simple. It took them 18 needles just to freeze the area of my cheek where the restoration was to happen. I had no idea what was going on except that so far nothing was happening to my rear end. There had obviously been a change in plan. The cancer would be removed in some other way.

An hour and a half and 125 stitches later — with a huge, heart-shaped, puffy, still-bleeding scar on my face — I said to Eric, the plastic surgeon who had performed

16

this neat piece of work: "So what have you done?"

"It's a new procedure that I learned a couple of weeks ago in Paris," he said, "I thought I'd try it out on you."

"Thanks heaps," I said.

Eric told me that despite the initial blood and gore, the scar would heal, that in a few months I would be very happy, and that in a year or so the scar would be all but invisible. The V-flap operation, he said, would be much better in the long run than affixing the skin from my rear, which because of its unique pigmentation would remain forever butt white.

Round One appeared to be a success, but a bigger test was yet to come. The medical team was not 100 per cent sure that they had removed all of the cancer. I would have to go to the Vancouver Cancer Clinic for further examination by a 10-doctor team — a conference to determine whether or not a second operation would be required. The thought of it was terrifying.

I should tell you right now that despite a constant, not-too-enthusiastic fight against flab, I have really enjoyed a healthy life. No hospitals, except to visit others; no operations, no anaesthetics. Another operation, I quickly concluded, would introduce me to everything all at once. I might never be the same again. Worse than that, I would probably die. Again, my mind was skidding me straight to the morgue!

Whoa there, Pete! How about the skills of the doctors? The technology? We all have special talents, don't we? Could it be that whatever they have in store for you has been done quite successfully hundreds of times to others? The surgical fight against cancers of all kinds has seen many incredible victories. Where's your faith and positive attitude? How about the love that's pouring out for you from your family and friends?

The doctors decided that the second operation was indeed required, and they set the date for seven and a half hours of surgery at Vancouver General Hospital.

Charlie Trimbell, who is president of Oppenheimer Bros., one of Western Canada's leading food brokers, and a good friend, told me: "Pete, you have pretty good people skills. When you get into hospital, put them into overdrive. Use your skills to get on the good side of everyone who comes into your room. Regardless of what they do, learn their names and try to find out what they do. It will be the beginning of greater understanding at an incredibly important time. The care you receive from doctors, nurses, orderlies will be more gentle because you will have given each of them something of yourself." I told him I would do my best.

I took in two boxes of my first book How to Soar With the Eagles and gave them away at every opportunity. No matter who came into my room, they got a signed copy of my book. Was I covering my aforementioned backside? You never know, do you?

As well as making all of these literary presentations, I talked at length to all of the people who were involved in my immediate hospital world, to all those who would be playing a role in my surgery the following day.

I paid special attention to the anaesthetist. Len was a warm, friendly, efficient and sensitive man from England. When he came to see me on the eve of my operation, I spent more time questioning him than all of the doctors and nurses together. I told Len that in the morning, just before he put me under, I wanted to gather all of the nurses and doctors around my bed and offer them a five-minute Legge motivational speech. Some last-minute insurance.

"Really?" said Len. "And what are you going to say?"

"What will I say? I will say: You doctors and nurses do this operation almost every day of every week. You are considered the best in Western Canada. You probably view this as just another neck dissection on just another body, but I'd like to tell you that for me, this is the first and ONLY time I'm going to have this operation. Today, you will be better in all of your functions than you have ever been before. Your skills will be superb. No side effects whatsoever. No mistakes. Just a smooth, well-performed, 100 per cent successful operation, the best you can possibly perform." I used every adjectival rouser in the book, my own and everyone else's!

"Great," said Len. "I'm looking forward to it."

The next morning at five, I was awakened by my nurse, who, not surprisingly, gave me pills to make me sleep. Then it was onto the trolley and off to the O.R. In there, all kinds of people were scurrying around, checking equipment, doing whatever it is that these green-gowned creatures do. Sharpening knives? Recovering from the night before?

I looked at the clock. It was 8:10 a.m. Time for the motivational. "O.K.," said Len. "Just one minor adjustment before you begin ..." and as he spoke a world of nothingness closed around me.

I looked at the clock again. It was 8:15. Five minutes later. Nope. It was twelve hours and five minutes later. No longer was I surrounded by the twilight of morning. There was pain, and a great city hospital went about its business in the darkness of a winter evening. The deed had been done. Things would be different, but I was very much alive.

Alive, but not necessarily the happiest of campers. Christmas was coming, and I knew that in this season of traditional celebration, when families invariably came closer together, I would stand out as a substantially scarred face in the family crowd. My cheek was swathed in dressings, but I knew that beneath it all, there was a different-looking husband, a different-looking dad, a different-looking guy who would be appearing in future bookings on the podiums of the world. Different looking and substantially broken inside.

Would there even *be* future bookings, I asked myself? Maybe I'd lost it. I tested my voice and it was little more than a croak. I moved in the darkness and several I.V.s followed me around, tugging painfully at my flesh. Could I ever swing a golf club again? I doubted it.

A lot of people have trouble visiting the sick in hospitals, especially those who come out looking different than when they went in. You have to steel yourself for these visits, attempt to disregard the smells, the foreign images. You have to say to yourself: "I'm going in here to make this person feel better, and no matter what I'm about to see in that bed, I won't flinch."

My family came early to see me and Kay and my three daughters *all* flinched. They caught themselves quickly, but they flinched. I'd never hold that against them. It's just one of those things that happens when you're shocked by an image you weren't expecting. I suspect that I looked pretty awful.

My eldest daughter, Samantha, dived in for the kill — and I'll always be grateful that she did. I can't remember her exact words but, whatever they were, she got them right.

"For years, Dad, you've talked about people who end up in situations like this, people who have been bruised and beaten, who for whatever reason, are hurt physically or mentally in life. And what you have said to them is that they must live for today and have hope for tomorrow . . . "

Both of us had tears in our eyes.

"Yes," I said.

"Now it's *your* turn to be the model. Now it's *your* turn to dig deep and draw on all of those things that you've said are important in life — courage, hope, love, the strength of the family. We'll be with you. No matter what."

"Yes," I said. "I know that."

"You're the one who always says that we must have goals and be able to visualize the things we want. Visualize your way out of here!"

The healing had begun. And I knew that while things had changed, the *best* things were still as they had always been. I could feel them all in that room.

The sun had come up, just like always.

And Christmas, wonderful Christmas, was just around the corner.

You can have

everything in life

if you help enough

other people to get what

they want in life.

— Zig Ziglar

CHAPTER 2

By Boat to New Beginnings

I THINK I SAID ELSEWHERE that as I grow older, I am no longer the lover I was (or *thought* I was!), but I love *more* than I once did. I believe that love, and our *understanding* of love, deepen as we grow older and grow in wisdom.

If we *want* it to be, love can be clouded by complications. As we age and grow in wisdom, love becomes more pure, more accessible. It takes less time to regenerate the power of love. We know it's there, we can return to it more quickly because we understand it better.

You think a lot about love when you're recovering from big surgery. That's not *all* you think about, but love is right up there with the other big things. A hundred times a day in a quiet hospital room you silently check your values. What have you done in life? How might you be remembered if you don't pull through? What is the sum of your parts — those that you still have!

You don't think a lot about bank accounts and net

worth. Somehow they don't seem too important. That's something for each of us to remember when we reassess life's priorities. You don't need money to love and be loved. You can't put a dollar value on love and hope, on friends and family.

Many people were extremely kind to me while I was in the hospital. The nurses said they had never seen so many flowers arrive so quickly. Some of the flowers I shared with patients in the ward who weren't so fortunate. Other flowers went home to make room for more. The walls were strung with cards of encouragement. Each message was a shot of adrenaline, a new touch of wellness.

I determined very early that despite some residual pain, and a neck and a chest that remained held together with staples, I wouldn't be in hospital any longer than I needed to be. If I was mending, it could be done as well at home.

Padding around the ward, I spoke to others, some who seemed to be veterans of hospital life. One patient, who had gone through almost the same operation I had, seemed a likely person to tell me how to make a quick hospital exit.

"What has to happen for me to leave this place?" I asked him.

"First, the I.V. has to go," he said.

"Check."

"Then the neck drain."

"Check."

"No more morphine."

"Check."

"No more catheter."

"Check."

"You must urinate four times before noon and the nurse must know it's happened."

"Check."

"You must go Number Two once before noon and the nurse must know it's happened."

"Check."

"And then you're out of here."

"So how are *you* doing?"

"Well, the I.V. has gone. So has the neck drain, the morphine, the catheter . . ."

"How about the others?"

"No problems. They've both been happening before noon."

"So why aren't you out of here?"

"I never wake *up* before noon!"

Notwithstanding the delays experienced by others, I was out of the hospital in three days. It was pre-Christmas, it was cold and wet, and home and hearth was the best place to be. I could shuffle around the familiar routes there much more comfortably than I could the shiny corridors of a hospital. There is no greater strength than that which comes from a loving family. I *looked* a mess, but I was on the road to rapid recovery. I knew my wife and daughters would speed the process even more.

Love was stronger and even better. Having been to the wall, I once again shuffled my priorities, adjusted my plans to match real or imagined circumstances.

And one thing that entered my planning was a holiday. A big one.

Twenty-five years ago, I was hired by the P&O

people to be an entertainer on a cruise ship. As a kid in his twenties, it was a heaven-sent gig that comes once in a lifetime. On board the good ship Oriana — then the queen of the P&O cruising fleet — I would do standup comedy every fourth night on a voyage from Vancouver to London. Tough life! During that voyage, I met a young lady who was returning from Vancouver to London to marry a gent called Tony. Somewhere in the vicinity of Jamaica, I suggested that she dump Tony and marry *me*. *She* did and *we* did, and Kay and I have been married ever since.

So having survived surgery for cancer and having reached the 25-year plateau in our marriage, we went to sea again — a journey on the Sky Princess from Fort Lauderdale in the middle of a Canadian winter. This time there were 27 of us in the party, including our daughters, parents, some very close friends, my partner Neil Soper and his wife Sharon. There are ten suites on the Sky Princess and we had five of them. Extremely expensive. No, I wasn't generous enough to pick up the tab for everyone. We played a lot, but we also recharged our batteries, put focus into our lives again, shared rewards that each of us had earned along the way.

There's something special about a ship that people wiser than I could talk about for days. Ships gather you in and hold you closer. I hope that no one is offended, but maybe that's why they often end up being feminine in gender.

I discovered a special love on a ship and went back to build again on that love. We leaned on the rail and looked out across a sparkling, moonlit sea. We remembered another time, and we planned anew.

Just before the trip, I sat in my office and wrote the following words. I don't claim to be a poet, but perhaps I am an incurable romantic. Kay said she will treasure the words as much as the trip.

If I Had To Do It All Over Again

I'd love you more,
I would show more patience,
I'd encourage you more, I'd wipe my
sink of toothpaste more, I'd make you feel
cherished more, I'd listen more, I'd make love
more, I'd put my clothes away more, I'd give you
more credit for our spectacular children, I'd show more
appreciation for your courage, tolerance, commitment,
understanding and determination to make this the best
marriage in the world. But most important of all, I'd
marry you all over again. You are simply the very
best woman, mother, lover, friend any man could
ever dream, hope or wish for. Happy 25th
Anniversary my darling, I love you very,
very much. All my love forever, your
devoted husband

November 23, 1993

Our doubts are traitors,

and make us lose

the good we oft might win

by fearing to attempt.

— William Shakespeare

CHAPTER 3

The $10 Million Ethics Questions

AS PUBLISHER of a weekly television magazine that lists the programs in our city, I sometimes take an advance look at what's coming up on the tube.

Along with everything else on television these days, there is a daily selection of enormously successful talk shows, controlled by small groups of people who have become something like folk heroes in our always-looking-for-a-star society.

They are clever people, and their success is constantly encouraged and supported — not just by us who watch their programs, but by the networks they serve, by the teams that back them up with research and ideas.

The most noticeable link between all of these people is that their programs reflect what I think are the most extreme values of our society, the raw edge of what we would normally think of as normal behaviour.

In one recent week, Donahue was offering advice on love based on the experiences of gigolos and prostitutes, Sally Jessie was talking to pregnant drug addicts, Oprah was into men dealing with anger, and Geraldo was talking to people running away from mobsters (who would presumably be nimbly picked off by mobster hit men as they left the studio!).

One of Donahue's programs later that week offered tips on seducing women — how to guarantee sex on the first date.

In our market, Donahue comes on right about when the kids come home from school. So a 16-year-old settles into his couch potato position and flicks on Donahue. Interesting stuff, says the kid, taking notes. And his date that night happens to be my 14-year-old daughter! About to go out with someone who has just learned about guaranteed sex on the first date!

Do television talk shows mirror the times, or do the times mirror the talk shows? Are these people and the ideas they present leading us in new and uncertain directions?

I tell my audiences that while some of this stuff is unavoidable, we need to make absolutely sure as parents that our children are not compromised by someone else's values.

Teaching values to our children is not the church's job, not the school's job, but *our* job — at home, where it all begins. This statement invariably gets crashing applause. (Is the applause inspired because we think it's a good idea, or because that's what we're all doing? What happens in *your* house?)

In their great book The Day America Told the Truth, researchers-writers Peter Kin and James Patterson presented some incredible statistics that reflect where much of our society sits today on questions of values.

Of their response group, they asked: Do you lie regularly? Ninety-one per cent said yes.

Would you lie to achieve an important business objective? Twenty-nine per cent said yes.

Have you done anything in the last year you're ashamed of? Twenty-five per cent said yes.

And they had some money questions. Good old motivating money!

If you could pick up a quick $10 million, would you abandon your family? Twenty-five per cent said bye-bye to their family.

Would you abandon your faith, whatever it might be? Another 25 per cent said yes.

Would you be a prostitute for a week? Twenty-three per cent said yes.

Give up your spouse? Sixteen per cent said yes. (My audiences invariably laugh at the give up your spouse question. It's a nervous laugh, and I will comment no further.)

Kill a stranger? Seven per cent said yes.

And then the same group was asked: Should we

teach values and ethics in our schools? Eighty per cent of these men and women who would plunder, rape and kill said: "Absolutely!"

So where do *you* sit in all of this?

I think it was Abraham Lincoln who said if he had eight hours to chop wood, he would spend six hours sharpening his axe. Wise man.

Learning how to live, like preparing to cut wood, takes time. Learning how to live takes a *lifetime*.

You can't be an observer of your life; you have to be a *participant*. The way I see it, my responsibility is not to be the best in the world, but to be the best I can be.

I'm not hung up on being the best speaker, the best publisher, the best anything. But I'm certainly committed to discovering and using all of the gifts that came with the Legge package to discover just how *far* I can go. I know that with the right values, focus and attitude, it's a long, long way. And there's no way I can fail.

We can't waste time in life. Given half a chance, most of us will live to be about 85 years of age. It sounds like eternity. But try thinking of it as just 4,420 weeks, just 30,940 days! Not so long, huh?

We can't keep *wasting* our days. As I keep telling people and telling myself: Make today a mini life. You'll be amazed at how much you can achieve, how many books you can read, how much you can really get done.

Respect *yourself!* Since the dawn of anything approaching personkind, more than 11 billion people have lived on planet Earth, and every one of them past and present — and yet to come — is unique. Absolutely unique. When you look into the mirror in the morning, you may not be entirely happy with what you see, but what you see is a reflection of a unique person with unique gifts, unique potential. You sir, ma'am, you are one of a kind! You deserve the best you can give yourself!

I respect and love life, and as often as I can I pump myself with the thought that I must live life to the full, fill the data bank that is my brain with all the knowledge it can handle.

I believe in the Olympic ideal — that I must work hard to achieve what I want to achieve, that gold medals in athletics or life don't come overnight.

I believe that I must always try, always attempt, no matter how small or large the task. I will make those calls, write those letters. I will simply try.

I believe that as well as trying, I must strive. I won't go along with the naysayers, with those who don't give a rip. I will dig down deep, to strive, to push myself.

And because of all this, I will support my promise to myself to be the best I can be.

Our value systems *are* changing. The Golden Rule of my youth was do unto others as they would do unto you. These days it seems to be do unto others so that they won't get a chance to do unto you. Why the change? It goes against every principle of success. I have never got anywhere in life by dumping on anyone, by pushing to the head of the line, by *taking* to achieve my goals. Conversely, I have found that the more I give, the more I get back. Try it some time. Try it *all* of the time and you will see the beginning of a string of unbelievable and invariably rewarding miracles!

Walt Disney's brother Roy said when values are clear, decision-making is easy. I totally agree with him.

Technology has perhaps made the processes easier, but clear values can outstrip the fastest technology. YES, you will say or NO. The values you have within you leave no doubt as to where you stand. "Always let your conscience be your guide," said Jiminy Cricket.

People have been asked what they look for in a leader. What are the character traits they would best latch onto?

What they want more than anything else is honesty. They want to believe and trust what they hear. I agree. If you are a person of integrity and honesty, people will beat a path to your door.

The second thing they want is competence. Honesty first, competence second.

The third thing they want is a leader who can inspire them, who can look beyond today toward something better — the loftier goal, the higher road, the inspirational tomorrow.

Values are incredibly important and always have been. Ask Pete Rose or Richard Nixon, Leona Helmsley or Robert Maxwell. The evidence seems to indicate that

34

Maxwell, faced with a world of crumbling values, said that's it, and plunged into the sea. The end of an empire!

Without values, we can suffer the same kinds of consequences as all of these former giants. We can sink as low, or we can rise to the loftiest planes.

There is a great Stattler Brothers song about the aspirations of a class of kids that all graduated in 1957 with the highest ideals. It goes:

Tommy's selling used cars and Nancy's fixing hair;

Harvey runs a grocery store and Margaret doesn't care;

Gerry drives a truck from Sears and Charlotte's on the make;

And Paul sells life insurance and part-time real estate;

And the class of '57 had its dreams.

We all thought we'd change the world with our great works and deeds;

Or maybe we just thought the world would change to fit our needs;

Ah, but the class of '57 had its dreams.

Betty runs a trailer park and Jan sells Tupperware;

Randy's in an insane ward and Mary's on welfare;

Charlie took a job with Ford and Joe took Freddy's wife;

Charlotte took a millionaire and Freddy took his life.

Ah, but the class of '57 had its dreams.

A speaker friend of mine from Seattle tells about crossing the international border between Washington State and British Columbia. You are asked three questions as you move, usually in a minute or so, from one great country to the other.

Who are you? Where are you going? What do you have to declare?

These questions work well at the border because the answers can say so much.

They also work for life.

CHAPTER 4

Give, and It All Comes Back

THERE ARE SOME PHYSICAL LAWS and some laws of life that, no matter what happens, never change.

One of them is the Law of Gravity. I won't go into *why* it does what it does, because I don't *know* why it does what it does. All I know is that if you trip, chances are you'll fall; that if you tip a glass over at the edge of the table, it will hit the floor.

If you jump from the top of a tall building, unlike Superman, you won't fly. You will fall at 32 feet per second and increase your speed at that rate every second until you hit the ground. At which point, other principles of physics will become involved, causing horrible things to happen to your body. Don't try it, just believe me. The Law of Gravity dictates that young or old, rich or poor, tall or short, male or female, when it comes to jumping off buildings, we all travel at the same accelerating rate.

A great principle of *life* is that we reap in direct proportion to the rate that we sow. Sow bad, we reap a *harvest* of bad. Serve up misery, we get misery back. Smile. Some will look the other way because they think you're crazy. Most will smile back.

Give of yourself and the bounty that comes back will overflow the granaries of your life.

Before I tell you about my own experiences, let me tell you about the observations of others on the issues of giving and serving.

Zig Ziglar, North America's foremost motivational trainer, whose name is as strange as my own, says you can get everything you want in life if you help enough people get what *they* want in life. Keep giving, you keep getting.

Zig is not suggesting that you should give with an expectation of getting something back. What he's saying is that a *law* comes into play when you give of yourself, and what comes back is *automatic.* Just as *gravity* is automatic. You can't turn it off.

Canadian lecturer Brian Tracy has produced a best-selling series of audio tapes that he calls The Universal Laws of Success and Achievement. While he brings things up to date, many of the universal laws are developed from observations that had already been made by some of the great thinkers of the ages many years before.

These never-changing laws, some of which go back as far as 4,000 years, can become guideposts for life's highway. They can be the bright and shining rules for the conduct of our short lives, to help us maximize success, to help us enjoy ourselves, fulfill ourselves in the richest possible ways.

The great Law of Cause and Effect says that you and I live in an orderly world in which everything happens for a reason. Sometimes it doesn't seem quite that way, but it is. There are no accidents.

It's no accident that many men and women around the world enjoy a unique level of success by giving back to the community that gave to them.

An infatuated fan once told Mother Theresa that he intended to follow her around the world to see what she did and how she did it — to learn her secrets first hand. He bought a plane ticket and was about to embark with her on a trip to South America, another leg in her world-wide, lifelong mission of service. Mother Theresa was flattered, but said simply: "Sell your ticket. Give the money to the poor."

What an incredible lesson that man learned in those seconds. We can line up to shake the hands of kings, queens, prime ministers and movie stars and probably learn nothing. Those same kings, queens, prime ministers and movie stars line up to meet Mother Theresa. Mother Theresa says *give,* then goes her quiet way. And we stand in open-mouthed wonder to ponder her wisdom.

I believe that despite the depressing news on Page One, we are becoming a more serving world. We are dis-covering that while we may feel a momentary rush to accumulate wealth, there comes a time in the exercise when wealth for wealth's sake becomes a burden, when it's time for less of self, more of service to others.

It's not complicated. As others have said: "Just do it." Find a cause that interests you or a charity that could use your gifts and talents and offer yourself, no strings attached.

Twenty years ago, I made a decision to give back to the community something of what the community gave to *me.* I genuinely wanted to serve someone else. Not to get something back, but, through the things I might be able to do, to give something that was giveable from *my* life.

And just as it happened for others, the benefits that came back to *me* have far exceeded anything I might have given. Like the Law of Gravity, it has just *happened.*

I began doing what I did because of my father, Bernie Legge, who has spent his Canadian lifetime giving to and serving dozens of organizations. He is my life role model for unselfish service, and in his home town of New Westminster, B.C., his basement walls are decorated with dozens of plaques, awards, certificates and trophies that recognize his many years of community involvement.

Perhaps his proudest moment came in 1989 when the City of New Westminster named him Citizen of the Year. He can reflect today not just on that award, but on every award he has received — and the riches that each has left in his heart.

My twenty years of service have also brought me recognition, and I'm as proud as my Dad is in the profound worth of this list:

ORDER OF VARIETY

Presented at the Variety Club Global Convention in Chicago, 1988, in recognition of outstanding support of Variety Club International projects on behalf of children with special needs.

MARKETING EXECUTIVE OF THE YEAR - 1991

Presented by the Sales and Marketing Executives in recognition of outstanding achievement in the field of sales and marketing.

PAUL HARRIS FELLOW AWARD - 1991

Presented by Rotary International in recognition of excellence as a communicator and motivator.

THE SOVEREIGN ORDER OF ST. JOHN OF JERUSALEM

Inducted as a knight in 1992. This prestigious global benevolent association is dedicated to public service.

VARIETY CLUB MEDIA AWARD - 1993

Presented February 14, 1993. The Variety Club of British Columbia "Show of Hearts" Media Award was presented in recognition of 16 years of outstanding support of the annual Variety Club Telethon and British Columbia's Special Kids.

COMMONWEALTH MEDAL FOR THE 125TH ANNIVERSARY OF CANADIAN CONFEDERATION

Presented March, 1993. Awarded by His Excellency The Right Honourable Ramon John Hnatyshyn to Canadians who have made a significant contribution to their country, community and fellow Canadians.

ORDER OF SAINT LAZARUS OF JERUSALEM

Inducted in 1993. Recipients are nominated because of distinguished service to God and country and pledge support by effort and alms to the Order's works of mercy and charity.

TOASTMASTERS INTERNATIONAL - 1993 GOLDEN GAVEL AWARD

Presented to a worthy individual who has distinguished him or herself in the field of communication and leadership and in recognition of contributions to the art and science of communication. Previous recipients include Dr. Robert Schuller, Art Linkletter, Walter

Cronkite, Tom Peters, and others of substantial international reputation. I was overwhelmed by the honour!

The ceremony for the Variety award in 1988 took place in Chicago's Soldier Museum; the gala black tie affair was attended by hundreds of delegates from around the world. My acceptance speech included a borrowed story from Dale Galloway's masterful 1975 book Dream a Dream. It went something like this:

Little Chad was a shy young kid, and one January day he came home and told his mother that he would like to make a Valentine card for everyone in his class.

Her heart sank. "I wish he wouldn't do that," she thought. She watched the children when they walked home from school, and Chad was always at the end. The others laughed and clung to each other. Chad was never included.

But she went along with his wish, bought the paper, the glue and the crayons, and night after night for three weeks, Chad painstakingly made 35 Valentine cards.

On the big day, Chad was beside himself with excitement. He stacked the cards, put them in a bag and bolted out the door.

When he came home that night she would have cookies and milk waiting for him. They might ease the pain, because she sensed there would be few cards for Chad that day, perhaps none at all.

That afternoon the cookies and milk were on the table when the children came home. Through the window she could see them and, as always, Chad was in the rear.

He came inside and, while his arms were empty, his face was aglow.

"Not a one," he said. "Not a one. I gave them all away."

Life's greatest joy is not to get, but to *give* love away.

There are words that go: "It isn't a song until it's sung, it isn't a bell until it's rung and it isn't love until it's given away."

I treasure the honours that have come to me in life. But nothing has been more rewarding than being able to give of myself to earn them.

Try it. Try it today.

Insanity has been defined as doing the same things in the same way and expecting to get different results.

— Anonymous

CHAPTER 5

It's YOU Who Changes Things

WHEN MY FATHER WAS 16, he told his parents that he was going to run away to sea. It was February, 1928. In the timeline of world history, it was not too long ago, but considering what has happened since then, it seems Jurassic. Suffice it to say that out there, beyond that village near Cardiff in Wales, there was indeed a world of enormous opportunity.

As a sailor in the merchant marine, in ships that make international trade possible, Bernie Legge circumnavigated planet Earth nine times in voyages that I know opened his eyes and gave him much wisdom.

Twenty years later, he left the merchant marine and was married. And still restless for a home over the horizon, he remembered from his travels Vancouver, British Columbia. It was forty years ago when he followed his dream.

When I tell Dad's story in presentations around the world, I sometimes pause at that point, and, as the house lights come down, the music comes up and Louis Armstrong's Wonderful World accompanies a visual presentation of the sights of Vancouver. But they are not glamour pictures. They are pictures of another side of the city, of the lonely and the lost, of the bag people, the people who live under bridges and in doorways downtown. They are the people who seem to have lost their dreams.

When the song ends and the house lights come up, I tell my audiences that 80 per cent of the things we see and think about are negative. Our media is negative, we too often view our fellow human beings negatively, we're negative about our jobs and negative about our country.

I say that if we subscribe to the fact that we become what we think about most of the time, we can easily end up being extremely negative people.

And I say there's no reason to be this way when there is such opportunity within each of us to be the most passionately positive people anywhere in the world.

When I go to a foreign country, I often meet Canadians who invariably seem to identify themselves with maple leaf lapel pins or maple leaf knapsacks, or maple leaf anything!

Out there in the big world, they advertise their enormous love for Canada, proudly tell the story of this great country to absolutely anyone who will listen. No longer are they in the economic or social shadow of the United States, no longer are they 'God's frozen people,' no longer are they 'hosers' or part of a collection of boring non-achievers that so many of us often think we are. They are passionate and positive people who love their land.

Canada and all Canadians are respected around the world as kind, generous, caring, hard working, diligent people — along with dozens of other adjectives that describe the incredible coast-to-coast collection we are. I revel in the adoration. I believe in Canada and I urge my audiences to do the same, to get excited about Canada. I tell them in no uncertain terms that if we *don't* start believing, Canada, by our collective negativism, can go down the tubes.

Canada is a magnificent land, an incredible land where, despite any short-term economic hiccups, dreams *can* be realized.

I was in Ottawa early in 1993 for a national prayer breakfast, the guest of Senator Ray Perrault. Politicians, senators, judges, ambassadors and others came together in the Confederation room and prayed together for Canada. It wasn't a prayer for a boat about to go down. It was because all of those people believed passionately about this country and believed in prayer as a means of getting in touch with a greater power, bigger than all of them, to share their pride and their love of Canada. It was sincerity, not cynicism. "You're out there, God. Thanks for all of this. Stick with us as we stumble along together."

Where there is no vision, people perish. Entire cultures have disappeared because the dream was never there, the house was built without a foundation and the winds of the world blew it away.

We will always be tested. We survive the storms of life when our values are firmly rooted, when we understand that we can't compromise on things like honesty and integrity, with our mates, with our children, with everyone who comes in and out of our lives.

I make a point in my presentations with a silly, unlikely story about Michelangelo, who dropped his paintbrush one day while working on the ceiling high in the Sistine Chapel.

"I'll be damned," he said.

Below, a nun saw and heard him. "We don't use language like that in here," said the nun. "All we say is praise the Lord!"

Suitably admonished, Michelangelo made his way down to retrieve the brush. Halfway down, the scaffold began to fall.

"Praise the Lord!" he shouted. And the scaffold stopped in its tracks and returned to where it had been.

"I'll be damned," said the nun.

A ridiculous story, but a fun one. Our bigger lesson from the incredible Michelangelo is that despite the enormous and spectacular contribution he made to the world in his art, his sculpture, his poetry, he always said: "And yet, I am still learning."

I don't know about you, but I value *today* above all others. I make every presentation as if it were my last because, while it may not be likely, I say to myself why *not* go flat out? Won't that kind of positive thinking make it a *better* presentation? Why go in with something less than great? Great athletes don't do it, great businesspeople don't do it. Being honest with yourself means giving it your best shot, building the best foundation for the job, playing to win.

I value the present, I'm passionate about life, about my country. I'm passionate about my goals, my company, about the men and women who share my goals. I know that the storms of life will test us all.

Being too round and too short, I may never be a great basketball player, but I sure as heck can be just about anything else I want to be. Like you, I was born implanted with the seeds of greatness, of success. That's not a pompous bit of hot air, it's *true!*

I may challenge and stimulate with my books and presentations, but I can't do much about motivation. It's *you* who must motivate you.

How, when and where you live your dreams is dependent on what *you* put in your mind.

In school, I was a non-achiever. I was in the half of the class that made the top half possible. But along the way I learned from motivational speaker Charlie "Tremendous" Jones that you are influenced and changed by just three important things: the books you read, the people you meet, the places you go.

Our minds, like plants, are for nurturing. I'm told that giant bamboo trees show no visible signs of life for the first five years. But you tend the plant, care for it, fertilize it and in the fifth year, it explodes out of the ground. It grows a foot a day and, in no time at all, it's close to 100 feet high. Did it do all of that in a year? Or did it take five years? Was that great spurt in the fifth year a manifestation of all of the caring that had gone before?

Lives are years, but they are also months, weeks and days, even hours and minutes. We need to count our lives in days to give urgency to our purpose. We need to look on our days as mini-lives. We don't have to kill ourselves with work or kill others in our scramble for the top, but nor can we let our days slip by without adding something to our lives, to the lives of others.

We don't lack resources in Canada. But, too often, those of us who live here lack resourcefulness.

On a remarkable visit to Israel, a state I'd recommend to everyone who is looking to connect yesterday's history with today's vitality, I visited the Yad Va Sham Memorial in the holy city of Jerusalem. Part of the Memorial recalls Hitler's rise to power, to explain the madness of his mission. Another part of it is the children's museum. You enter by walking down a ramp into darkness. Guided by a handrail, you look up at what seems to be a night sky filled with millions of stars.

Sound? All you can hear are the voices of a man and a woman. They are reading names. The name, the age and the country of birth of the children who died in the Holocaust. It takes about three minutes to go through the building and the names never stop.

I later learned that if the tape of these names were to run 24 hours a day every day, it would take two years before the names would be repeated.

What grief. What perspective. What a way to bring yourself back to what you have, what you *can* have, to the urgency of living life.

After visiting that building, there is really no way that you can ever complain again.

I came to Canada with my family when I was twelve. The Second World War had ended, and we had the good fortune to survive it. During the war, as Germany threatened to annihilate a generation, thousands of children were sent from London into the country, to other countries, to be safe from what might come. It was a grand plan, but as with so many grand plans, it was full of tragedies.

You can read about all of it in cartoonist Ben Wicks' great book No Time to Wave Goodbye.

Ben tells one story in his book about a nine-year-old girl and her five-year-old brother who were shipped out of London. Hundreds of parents and children were at the station. The departure was made on a flood of the tears of hundreds.

"Whatever happens," said the mother to her little girl, "never let go of your brother's hand."

For six hours they rode a train north from London, two small and confused children on a terrifying ride to nowhere.

At the end of the ride, all of the children would be paired with new guardians, some good, some horribly bad. The girl and the boy, holding hands at the end of the long platform, were the last to be chosen.

An elderly couple took them home, fed them, put them to bed. There were two camp cots, one child in each. In the dark of the room, the burden of the day had mounted. They were alone and afraid. The girl could still hear her mother's voice. "You are responsible for your brother. Hold his hand."

In the dark, she made her way to her brother's bed and climbed in. She prayed for her country, for peace, for her parents, her foster parents downstairs. And in the darkness, her heart breaking, she began to cry. So as not to wake her brother, she buried her face into his pillow and the tears kept coming.

And then a hand, the small hand of her brother, reached out in the darkness to find hers.

"I'll take care of you," he said. "I'll take care of you."

We all need encouragement from time to time. Self motivation is tough. I imagine that all those years ago, my Dad had moments when he doubted the wisdom of his move to this land, when there were seemingly insurmountable difficulties.

I've certainly had them. Like you, I sometimes despair at how painfully we progress as a nation, how we keep making the same mistakes along the road to glory.

But I have learned that things can change, that things can *be* changed. We all have that capacity.

Think about Michelangelo, about the nurturing of bamboo. Think about the children of the Holocaust. You can't *take* life. Our obligation and our joy is to *live* it.

CHAPTER 6

Run With the Lions!

LET ME PREFACE THIS CHAPTER by saying that I have absolutely nothing against goats. Goats are cute and I very much like the rich and unique cheese that is made from their milk.

I also tell what I think is a short and very funny story about goats and their alleged tendency to eat just about anything that's lying around. Phone books, I'm told, are a particular favourite.

The joke? There were a couple of goats on the back lot at Universal Studios. One had its head in a can and was munching its way through the second reel of a movie.

"So, what do you think?" asked a second goat.

Speaking through a mouthful of celluloid, the first goat answered: "Not bad, but I liked the book a lot better."

The problem with goats is that, because they eat movies and do other silly things, they have earned a reputation for being basically stupid. That reputation has been transferred to what might appear to be the silly side of us humans.

"Don't be such a goat," we are told, and we know exactly what it means.

So now that you know I have nothing against goats except a belief in their collective earned reputation, let me get on with the bigger story.

A small and rather frightened lion cub ventured away from a protective pride of lions one sun-drenched Serengeti afternoon and wandered by chance and very nervously into a herd of goats.

Too small to look on them as food and too frightened to leave, the lion cub stayed. Nurtured and befriended by the goats, in time he became one with them. He walked, talked and smelled like a goat — even munching from time to time on Serengeti phone books.

But things were to change.

One sunny afternoon, he walked with the goats to drink at a bright and shiny, newly-filled waterhole. And as he drank, he saw his reflection and realized for the first important time that he was not a goat. His colour, his shape, his size — most everything about him — was quite different from the animals drinking beside him.

His ears went up to points, the goats' ears hung low. He had a mane and whiskers galore round his face, but no beard. Hmmm, thought the lion who had until then thought of himself as a goat. Hmmm, indeed.

As happens in stories like this one, his life was to change with dramatic suddenness. From a thicket nearby came a bounding, snarling, ferocious, muscular, huge lion obviously intent on a lunch of prime goat. In a flash, the goats scattered, running for their lives.

No big deal, thought the lion cub. Whatever it is, that creature is certainly big, certainly noisy, certainly impressive. But all things considered, it looks just about the same as I do.

The big lion roared in frustration at a missed kill and the lion cub roared, too. And future territorial battles notwithstanding, the two lions met, sniffed, nudged and recognized immediately that they were both of the same spectacular species.

The big lion turned and began to walk away.

"Come with me," he said. "You're not one of them, you're a lion. Come with me and live like a lion. You have been given strength and intelligence that is far beyond the strength and intelligence of a goat. Come with me and live like a lion."

The cub hesitated for a moment, looked briefly in the direction of the fleeing goats, then turned and did indeed follow the lion. He *was* a lion and he would live like a lion.

Thank you goats, he said, looking back for one more brief moment, but it's *au revoir!*

All of us, especially when we're younger, land from time to time in the wrong place. Our world and the societies and individuals within it, offer hundreds of temptations that get us off track — and suddenly we're in there with the goats.

Short-term benefits? Maybe. A quick hit, a quick buck, a quick thrill — the goats offer each in all shapes and sizes. Try this, do that, go for this, go for that. The goat road is always open, and for a while it's a real buzz.

But what happens in the morning? What happens after the first thrill? Is there a second? A third? And what's at the end of the road? Most often a sign that says NO EXIT.

From time to time, we see a light and cuddle up to the first affectionate goat — a metaphor that can be extended into every conceivable corner of our lives. But we don't have to stay. We can make choices, and we don't have to wait forever for a strong and bounding lion to lead us back. We can do it ourselves.

Have you ever thought what your potential might be if you *really* began to set and meet some self-improving goals? You want to accumulate money and be a millionaire? It starts by learning some of the rules, by foregoing short-term spending on things you probably don't need anyway for the satisfaction you will get by learning about saving, about wise investing. Believe me, there *is* no other way.

Have you thought what your potential might be if you said *no* to television a little more than you do now and dived into the wealth of learning that books provide?

If you spend one hour a day reading the right books, listening to the right tapes, adding to that great data bank that is your marvellous brain, you can change your life any way you want to change it.

We are born with nothing more than a fear of noise and a fear of falling. That's all. Everything else is acquired. As babies and infants, the messages we get are largely directed by others. But at some stage in our lives, what we gather as information is directed by *us.*

There is such an enormous opportunity for each of us to do things that reflect just how brilliant we are, just how superbly crafted we human beings can be.

Someone once said that if an entire world generation lived on the best of biblical principles, the world overnight would be free of war, of hatred, of everything that seems now to keep us in turmoil. Incredible, isn't it? What a glorious possible dream.

But everything happens one person at a time. And that's you. Say goodbye today to the metaphoric goats and follow the lions to higher ground. It's what you are. It's where you can be.

Sow a thought and you reap an act;

sow an act and you reap a habit;

sow a habit and you reap a character;

sow a character and you reap

a destiny.

— Philosopher

CHAPTER 7

On Death and Not Dying

AS ANYONE WHO HAS BEEN THROUGH a near death experience will tell you, it's beautiful, it's frightening and it's very real.

The stories vary depending on the teller, but a common thread runs through them all. There is invariably a feeling of departure from one's body, of travelling upwards, often through tunnels of light, into more light beyond. People say they are very conscious of what's going on. They can "look down" at a scene that often includes themselves, at grieving relatives and friends, at accident scenes, at whatever "killed" them. They remain ambivalent, there is no real sadness for those "left behind" — there is no apprehension about what may lie ahead. Conversely, the prospect of some kind of a journey is altogether exciting.

But death doesn't happen. It's *near* death — and at some stage in this strange journey, the life factors take over and again begin to rule the brain. "Whoa," these people say to themselves, "what's happening here? This is not for me. I think I'm dying and right now I think I should be *living!* Gotta get back!" And in the twinkling of an eye, the heavenly choir stops singing; the lights go out, and they're back where they came from.

It's not an experience that's soon to be forgotten. As a matter of fact, it's an experience that never really leaves those who have had it. They tell the story over and over again, usually with a look on their faces that suggests they've been in the presence of something far beyond this earth, beyond anything we are normally able to comprehend. They have been changed. They say that the thought of dying no longer worries them, that when death comes for real, they will willingly do it all again.

The most important thing is that having gone through it, each seems to have a better understanding of what *life* is all about; how precious it is, how none of us can afford to waste a minute of the time that's been allotted to each of us. People who have been near death start doing things they never did before; they get to the point much more quickly, get on with things, make better, faster choices. They're a joy to be around.

I tell a story about a young boy who helped to support his destitute family by selling papers on a street corner in Chicago. In hot summers and frigid winters, he was there morning and evening, desperately pushing the news at any pedestrian and any motorist who would buy.

One mid-winter morning, with snow and sleet driven off the lake by a frigid wind, with the temperature at minus thirty, he was having little success. In three hours of numbing discomfort, he had sold no papers.

Disheartened and deadened by the cold, he was

ready to pack it in when a block-long, black limousine pulled up beside him, the back window went down, a hand came out and a voice shouted: "Your papers, kid. I'd like all of them!"

The boy was shaken into instant warmth. "Huh?"

"I want to buy all of your papers. And hop in, I'll give you a ride home."

Hmmm, thought the boy, this isn't in the script. First, a stranger buys all my papers and now he's offering me a ride home in a big black limousine?

But the sale, the offer of a ride and a lot of assurance of safety won out over the cold, and the boy piled into the warm car.

The stranger gave instructions to the driver, the boy's exact address.

"How did you know?" asked the boy.

On the way they stopped for food, then continued on. The stranger carried the food from the car, heading directly for the apartment where the boy lived, five floors up a dark, cold stairway.

"How did you know?" asked the boy.

"How did you know?" asked his mother.

"When I was your age," said the stranger, "this was my street and this was my apartment. This is where I decided that I would change my life."

True story? I have no idea, but like so many similar stories, it says that we can all change our circumstances, inject our minds with something better, make more of the time that's allotted to us.

I have no doubt at all that, in every sense of the word, near death is a fantastic experience. But I would hate to think that each of us must go through it to rekindle the latent, smoldering spark that's inside each of us.

Success, say those who are successful, is nothing more than the pursuit of a worthy ideal. Success isn't scratching and winning, it's chasing a goal with determination and winning a bit at a time. It's deciding, whenever you want, to leave the old, cold neighbourhood and head for the sun.

The best miracle is the one of your own making. When one comes along — and it certainly will — you'll feel it. Warm and wonderful.

CHAPTER 8

Doing It The Peale Way

ON A RECENT TRIP TO NEW YORK, I visited the 93-year-old Norman Vincent Peale Marble Collegiate Church on West 29th Avenue. Dr. Peale was one of North America's most beloved, motivational and inspirational ministers.

As I sat through the service, I was reminded of two of Norman Vincent Peale's words that together made one short, powerful, motivating sentence.

"Do it," he said. "Do it!" Long before Nike made the expression the buzz phrase of another, later generation, Dr. Peale said: "Do it!"

Got an idea? Do it! A great impulse, a burning desire? For goodness sake, do it!

We've ALL had a great idea. In the middle of the night, turning on a tap, sitting in front of the tube, at the movies, an idea comes. An idea to revolutionize the way something is done, an idea that can become the better mousetrap that will motivate millions to beat a path to your door.

So what do you do about it? You think about it, pick it apart until it can no longer stand on its own two firm feet. You find flaws in it, you find reasons why you shouldn't do it. You say nah, it's not that great anyway. And six months later someone from Des Moines, Iowa is on the cover of Time magazine with a widget that looks exactly like the stuff of your great idea. Drat! Why didn't I …?

You have no one to blame but yourself. YOU could have been the star on the cover of Time. All you had to do was do it. Get on with it. Believe in yourself. Take your great idea just as far as you could take it.

Remember how good you felt when you had your great idea? Charged up. Ready to go. Remember how awful you feel now, knowing that someone else did what YOU could have done?

You are the only one who can make the fortunes of your life change. It's you — you have to do it. YOU must set your goals, YOU must fulfill them.

There is little satisfaction in saying: "That was MY idea. I could have done that. I had drawings of a thing JUST like that. I could have produced one of those." But you didn't.

Luckily, the great ideas keep on coming.

Thomas Edison had more than a thousand patents to his credit. Telegraph, the development of telephones, incandescent lighting, the phonograph, electric generating equipment, 35mm celluloid film that introduced a new era of movie entertainment. Big stuff! Edison *did it,* again and again.

O.K., so we may not all have the inventive genius of

an Edison, but we owe it to ourselves to take hold of our best ideas and do something about them.

Dr. Peale said: "Got a great idea? Do it!" A dream? Do it. Ambition? Do it. Great impulse, burning desire? For goodness sake, do it!

What IS more important than action in a moment of opportunity? What indeed?

Do it! And let me know what you did!

Circumstances do not

make the man;

they merely reveal

him to himself.

— Epictetus

CHAPTER 9

Remembering Pearl Harbor

"FUNNY THING, WAR," said a cynical, satirical British comedy group back in the Sixties.

Not funny at all, of course. As Benjamin Franklin, who dropped much wisdom into history, said: "There never was a good war or a bad peace." Right on, Ben!

Unfortunately, the human race has forever mongered at war. And from it, all we seem to learn is that we should begin warring all over again — for territory, pride, power and any number of other reasons that are even more difficult to comprehend.

I know of no occasion when making war was ever the right decision.

On a speaking trip to Honolulu a year ago, I went to Pearl Harbor for the first time to reflect for a minute or two on war, specifically to go aboard what remains of the U.S.S. Arizona, sunk by the Japanese in a surprise attack on the Hawaiian Islands on December 7, 1941, and serving today as a monument to the folly of it all — a gigantic tombstone above the watery graves of those who died inside it.

At the site, it's all very organized. Tourists by the hundreds of thousands go there every year, drawn by who knows what. The unreality of it all a half century later? Morbid curiosity? For the same reason that we slow down when we pass traffic accidents on highways?

It's certainly not Disneyland. It's a place that stirs emotions in us, like any memorial, that rarely surface, that hush our voices, that inspire big, searching questions.

The irony of Pearl Harbor today is that many of the people who find their way there are Japanese people, the children and grandchildren of the generation who flew in on that distant Sunday morning to wreak maximum havoc on an unsuspecting U.S. naval base, who would draw the United States into the Second World War and, in due course, would feel vengeance from the terror of the atomic bomb.

I can only presume that the Japanese — now firmly entrenched in Hawaii in so many economic and other ways — go there for the same reasons that I did. To reflect on it all. To ask themselves why it happened, to regret, to forgive, to mourn, to *remember* Pearl Harbor.

At the site of the Arizona Memorial, people give you a sheet that asks for comments on various aspects of your visit — much like the research forms that pop up from time to time in restaurants and other places.

There's a spot for the tour number and, if you wish, your name, age and address. There's a section for comments, complaints and suggestions, each accompanied by little 'happy face' graphics. Under headings of Needs

Improvement, Satisfactory and Excellent, they ask what you thought of the visitor centre and museum, the bookstore, the snack shop, the film centre, the talk, the navy boat, the memorial, and "other." The whole thing is written in two languages: English, and perhaps not surprisingly, Japanese.

In June 1985, a woman — maybe a girl — named Deborah C. Sheldon wrote some verses about Pearl Harbor. They are there at the site and I wrote them down. We must remember the Pearl Harbors of the past. We must have hope, always, for the future.

> *Barnacle-hulled she sleeps*
> *In her cradle six fathoms deep*
> *A monument now where the fish feed*
> *And a rainbow blood she bleeds.*

> *Where are the Captain and crew*
> *The gallant, stouthearted and brave*
> *In silence the booty, the sacrifice bought*
> *Are they mute in their watery grave?*

> *Hansen, Hampton, Menefee*
> *Wherein lies your victory?*
> *Think not we're enslaved in the depths of the sea*
> *We're alive, alive, where hearts rest free.*

We are more than half

of what we are

by imitation.

The great point is

to choose good models

and study them

with care.

— Lord Chesterfield

CHAPTER 10

Towering Above All Else

GOODNESS KNOWS exactly why we build them, but towers — especially those with stairs and elevators that get us to the top — are wonderful things.

Needles of steel and concrete, they soar close to the clouds and often reach beyond them. They are magnificent symbols of our collective aspiration to reach for the stars.

I checked the Guinness Book of Records and discovered that way back in 2650 B.C., they had the same desire to go a little higher than the surrounding countryside. The Djoser step pyramid, the earliest known, was built in Saqqåra, Egypt. Complete with its limestone casing and very firm foundation, it reached a very respectable 204 feet.

From there, as dreamers dreamed and technology improved, towers and buildings through the ages pushed ever upward. The spire of St. Paul's Cathedral, made of lead-sheathed wood and built between 1315 and 1561, was a giddy 489 feet.

The Eiffel Tower, made of iron and built between 1887 and 1889 for the Paris exhibition, was 985 feet, 11 inches tall. It's a bit higher these days, with the addition of a TV antenna.

The tallest self-supporting tower in the world is the CN Tower in Toronto, which rises to 1,822 feet, 1 inch. Excavation for the 130,000-ton structure began on February 12, 1973, and it was topped off April 2, 1975. The workmen who built it said that it was ice — not wind, rain or snow — that worried them as they worked up there above the city and Lake Ontario. One slip could ruin your whole day! Guinness says that lightning strikes the tower about 200 times a year, and presumably rattles the dishes *and* the diners in the restaurant at the top.

There's a big tower in Moscow, way up there at 1,771 feet, and others of similar stature in Tokyo and Sydney.

The tower in Calgary, Alberta was originally called the Husky Tower. I presume it took its name from an oil company — which probably took its name from a dog. That tower was completed in 1968 and stands proudly next to the Palliser Hotel right downtown.

Calgary Tower is a member of the World Federation of Great Towers that includes, along with others I have mentioned, towers in London, Barcelona, Vienna, Canberra and Montreal. Remember that Montreal's was built as part of the Big O, when the city hosted the Olympic Games in 1976.

By world standards, the Calgary Tower I see often on speaking trips to Alberta is not one of the world's big-gies — a mere 626 feet. But the brochure they gave me when I went to the top said that it's as long as two football fields, that they used 140,000 tons of concrete to build it.

The amazing thing about all of that concrete is half of it is now invisible: the 70,000 tons that lie underground form the foundation for a 'building' that must withstand the tests of time, the cruel winds of winter, the snow, the sleet, the bone-chilling temperatures that hit the city between warm chinook winds, the searing heat of summer.

It's the same story with all of these tall towers. They begin with a very deep hole and a very firm foundation.

In Calgary there was no question about "if" or "when" rough weather would come. Weather of every conceivable kind was a given that would be part of the engineering. It would be built to withstand the worst.

I think that tower planning teaches us a great life lesson. Others, in colourful ways, have done the same.

U.S. President Abraham Lincoln said: "If I had eight hours to chop wood, I'd spend six hours sharpening my axe."

Jesus Christ told a great story about house building:

Everyone who hears my words and puts them into practice, is like a sensible man who builds his house on a rock. Down came the rain and up came the floods. The winds blew and roared upon that house. And it did not fall because its foundations were on a rock.

And everyone who hears my words, and does not follow them can be compared with a foolish man who built his house on sand. Down came the rain and up came the floods. The winds blew and battered the house until it collapsed and fell with a great crash.

If you read that parable from Matthew, Chapter Seven, you will quickly discover that there is never a suggestion that the storms are just a possibility. You can count on them to come. As surely as one low pressure system follows another, storms will come.

The people who designed the Calgary Tower didn't say: "Let's take a chance." Tower builders build for the worst of everything.

Everyday, we read about people losing their jobs. Newspapers, magazines, television and radio stations talk about how government and business is downsizing, dehiring, rightsizing, dismissing, terminating, letting go, offering golden handshakes, silver bullets, canning, adjusting. The fancy words all have the same effect — you're out of work.

After five, ten, twenty years people who were well trained to perform work that they thought would last a lifetime are suddenly on the breadline.

My question to these people — and excuse me if I sound a bit pompous — is: What have you been doing over the years to improve your skills or learn new ones to prepare yourself for an inevitable 'rainy day?'

In his new book Sharkproof, author, lecturer and businessman Harvey Mackay says that self-improvement is the one area where you should really increase and not decrease your spending. Take courses, he says. Upgrade your skills. You can't ever afford to rest on the skills you learned in high school or college.

Take it to the bank, dear reader: the rough times in life *will* come sooner or later. But with a greater depth of understanding, you will be able to weather the winds of change, move sideways into a new challenge, move upwards into new fields of opportunity. Maybe a hobby can be honed into a new career, a new field of entrepreneurship. Maybe with additional knowledge, your wild dream can be brought right into the mainstream of your life.

In the short term, you may end up on the street; but with energy, optimism and preparation, you can pick yourself up and start over.

Be prepared, said Lord Baden Powell. It is the motto of Boy Scouts around the world. Sharpen your axe before you cut the wood.

What are the blocks of the foundation of your life, your marriage, your relationship with your children now, those yet to come, your social and community responsibilities, your career, your changing careers?

Be prepared. You know you will thirst. Build a well now, so you may draw refreshing water for the heat that will come.

Nothing in this world

is so powerful

as an idea whose

time has come.

— Victor Hugo

CHAPTER 11

Everything in the Garden is Lovely

IN THE SUMMER OF 1986, Vancouver was host to evangelist Billy Graham.

Seven 'sold out' services were held at B.C. Place Stadium in downtown Vancouver and from all walks of life — young and old, rich and poor, of many spiritual and non spiritual beliefs — 40,000 people came each evening to hear the message of this world-famous spiritual leader. Expectations were always high, and I know that many in the crowds went away blessed with new energy, answers that would help them in life's great struggle.

One of my magazines, TV Week, carried an eight-page cover story on the Billy Graham Crusade, an event that would be televised later in cities across the country.

As a result of this media involvement, my wife Kay and I were invited to attend an intimate dinner with Mr. Graham and some of the key crusade people at the Hotel Vancouver before the Stadium event began.

We were seated next to David and Dorothy Lam. I

had heard of Mr. Lam, knew of the impact he had made over the years on the Vancouver community, but I had never met him. We hit it off tremendously.

Neither of us knew that night, that in a couple of years David Lam would become Lieutenant-Governor, representative in the Province of British Columbia of Her Majesty Queen Elizabeth. His appointment came on September 9, 1988. David See-Chai Lam was appointed Lieutenant Governor, following in the footsteps of great British Columbians like Walter Nichol, Eric Hamber, Walter Owen, Bob Rogers and Henry Pybus (Budge) Bell-Irving who, as a general in the Canadian Army in the Second World War, was one of the liberators of Amsterdam. It is a position of great honour.

David Lam grew wealthy developing real estate. With little fanfare, he seems to have given much of his wealth away in massive support for education, for the further beautification of British Columbia. He is a gentle man. In a recent magazine article, he was characterized by writer Peter C. Newman as being "totally void of any social pretensions."

It is quite possible that the relationship I developed with Mr. Lam since that first dinner happened because we are both public speakers. I speak professionally to almost 100 groups annually. On average, Mr. Lam makes one speech a day — and more than 300 in any given year.

Despite his gruelling schedule, David Lam wants to keep growing as a speaker. On a number of occasions, he has asked me to offer constructive advice on his skills. On two occasions, he has invited me to private luncheons with him and his wife Dorothy at Government House in Victoria. His people skills are exceptional, a wonderful mixture of warmth, grace and good manners. He's the right man at the right time for the job, and Her Majesty should be very proud.

One of the legacies Mr. Lam will leave when his posting ends are several new and rebuilt gardens at Government House, with others in the planning stage – some 21 gardens in all, plus six other projects related to the garden underway. After lunch on one of my visits, we toured the House and the Gardens and he showed me how it will all come together.

As well as the lunches, I have shared the speaking platform with Mr. Lam on a number of occasions. In May of 1992, he was to be there when I gave the keynote speech at the British Columbia Provincial Prayer Breakfast at the Vancouver Trade and Convention Centre. Along with Lieutenant-Governor and Mrs. Lam, the head table guests included British Columbia Premier Mike Harcourt, Vancouver Mayor Gordon Campbell, a number of representatives from the federal and provincial government and others.

Due to circumstances beyond their control, the Lams were unable to attend the annual prayer breakfast. But Mr. Lam did send a letter, and has given me permission to reprint it.

My wife and I regret that prior commitments in Victoria have denied us the pleasure of being with you today, as you meet to consider the importance of prayer and the spiritual dimension in the life of the individual and in our Province.

We have very much enjoyed in previous years the privilege of sharing this special occasion with you.

In speaking with you this morning, through your

Chairman, I would like to refer to one of the great joys in my life — that of tending a garden.

Our time in Government House has given me the opportunity to develop the naturalist within me. The House is most impressive, sitting on a hill overlooking the ocean about a mile to the south.

It has a lot of land, much of it in an undeveloped state; so I have initiated a project to create new gardens, upgrade existing areas and generally make the grounds more inviting, accessible and enjoyable.

When the project is complete, there will be a Victorian Rose Garden, an English Country Garden and a Wildflower Garden, in addition to other areas.

Many of the ideas for this project have come from Her Majesty's own gardens at Buckingham Palace and Windsor Castle. Knowing my interest, she was kind enough to show me those gardens during an audience with her not too long ago.

Gardens speak to us of growth, and of patience. The gardens at Government House constantly remind me of both. As they grow, they change and mature. Their colours vary from week to week.

Yet that growth and maturity is not accidental. It takes the patience of a guiding hand, the warmth of the sun and the refreshing rain to bring a garden to the place where it gives pleasure to those who wander through it.

So it is that we are cared for and tended by God who wants us to grow and mature, and to bring pleasure to those with whom we associate.

As we allow God to speak to us, as we seek to live out the values implanted within us by His spirit, we fulfill the best that He wants for us, in our home, at our work or school and in our community.

It is my hope, and that of my wife, that God will share His wisdom with you this morning through the words of Peter Legge.

I hope to be able to be with you and to greet you personally next year.

Gardens really *do* bloom with wonderful metaphors for life. We *are* like gardens. Our minds are like soil that can be enriched or poisoned. Minds don't have minds of their own. They return exactly what we put into them, shape who and what we become. One of us is a platform speaker, the other a Lieutenant-Governor of a great province. Both of us must feed our minds on the things that will ultimately move us toward our goals and dreams.

The good soil that each of us needs is very different. We may require a night school course, to read fifty books a year on our chosen profession (the average business person in North America reads just one!), to listen to motivational tapes, to listen to the wisdom of speakers like Brian Tracy, Zig Ziglar, Denis Waitley and others who come to our communities.

At the end of every gardening season, after the work, the enriching, the digging, the weeding, the learning, there is always a harvest. They are great days, and a well-tended garden offers great rewards. So too does life.

The mind is its own

place and in itself

can make a heaven

of hell, a hell of heaven.

— John Milton
Paradise Lost

CHAPTER 12

Convicted Drug Dealers will be Executed

THE BIG JETS HAVE DONE MUCH to shrink our world, but there are still many parts of it that seem distant. Discounting the usuals like Siberia, Patagonia and the polar regions, I still look upon Malaysia, Indonesia and much of South-East Asia as being off the beaten track. The Pacific Rim has become a social and economic collective in recent times but, despite this, it's still a long haul from North America to just about anywhere in the South Pacific and its neighbouring seas.

In 1992, I had the good fortune to be asked to make a presentation in Singapore, in the heart of all that distant geography. I looked forward to the trip, my first to that part of the world, with a great deal of excitement. We're often very ignorant of our world neighbours until we actually go there, walk the streets, listen to the sounds, try new tastes, smell the roses — or, in the case of Singapore, the orchids.

I knew Singapore only as a mixture of images and

fuzzy memories. They were of scratchy black and white newsreels from the Second World War, pirates in the Straits of Malacca, a place somewhere close to Borneo and somewhere south of Ho Chi Minh City. I remembered an economy that thrived on exotic goods like rubber, tin, tobacco and palm oil. A republic? A member of the British Commonwealth? Raffles? Cricket, pink gin and afternoon tea? I knew it was made up of a population of minorities who had taken hold of Singapore's strategic geography and built a centre of enormous financial and industrial power, with one of the highest standards of living, with some of the toughest *rules* for living just about anywhere.

At the end of the long trans-Pacific flight, I was met at the spectacular Singapore airport by an impressive immigration officer who gave me my first inkling as to why things really *are* so uptight in that part of the world.

Along with the usual welcome and smile was a stamped message that crunched into my passport with incredible clarity. "Convicted drug dealers," it read, "will be executed."

Now I'm not about to suggest that my trip to Singapore had anything to do with dealing in drugs, or that I felt threatened by the new stamp in my passport. Far from it. As I will reveal shortly, I'm one of the great drug "antis" and will remain so.

But being accustomed to the *laissez-faire* approach we have to things in general in most of North America, I was quite frankly blown away by the warning that in these parts, it's death for drug dealers.

"That's quite something," I said to the immigration officer. "Singapore really sounds like a no-nonsense place."

He smiled. "In Singapore," he said, "we have no drug dealers," and seemed as if he meant it.

I don't know whether or not some drug dealers take the risk and ply their trade in the back streets of Singapore, but in my brief visit to that amazing city, I did learn that the threat of very serious consequences really *does* seem to have a marked effect on the state of society and completely changes the way people go about their lives.

You don't deal drugs in Singapore and you don't drop your litter in public places. There are a hundred and one things you just don't do because — if you do — the law will get you with great intensity, all the way to execution with no questions asked.

Of course, there's a moral side to all of this. We North Americans defend with great vigor the rights and privileges we have built for ourselves over the years. Changes in the law, especially changes that remove real and perceived freedoms, come only after the longest debate. The law is there, and in most cases, it is upheld. But too often the wrong people seem to slip through the cracks in the law: the drug dealers and their lawyers find loopholes, crime increases, our freedoms are diminished at the hands of the law *breakers.*

Is the Singapore way the right way? Can we expect a greater degree of policing in North America's future to bring things back into line, or do we stumble along as we have always done and lump the consequences in with all of the other slings and arrows that threaten us?

Drugs are killers. Drugs usurp our energy, our creativity and our resources. Drugs destroy families and careers. In their insidious way, drugs lay down a blanket of brief comfort, then lift it to allow the cold, cruel winds of reality to blow even harder. Maybe execution of drug dealers *is* the way. It seems to be working in Singapore.

One Drug Awareness Week, I came across a piece of writing that I circulated among the staff at our company.

Like the law of Singapore, it too is tough. The metre and the language come out as something less than poetry, but I think it makes a point. I recognize the author, whoever he or she may be. It goes like this:

My name is cocaine, call me coke for short
I entered this country without a passport
Ever since then, I've made lots of scum rich
Some have been murdered and found in a ditch
I'm more valued than diamonds, more treasured
*   than gold*
Use me just once and you too will be sold
I'll make a schoolboy forget his books
I'll make a beauty queen forget her looks
I'll take a renowned speaker and make him a bore
I'll take your mother and make her a whore
I'll make a school teacher forget how to teach
I'll make a preacher not want to preach
I'll make you rob and steal and kill
When you're under my power you have no will
Remember, my friend, my name is "Big C"
If you try me one time you may never be free
I've destroyed actors, politicians and many a hero
I've decreased bank accounts from millions to zero
I make shooting and stabbing a common affair
Once I take charge, you won't have a prayer
Now that you know me, what will you do?
You'll have to decide, it's all up to you

The day you agree to sit in my saddle
The decision is one that no one can straddle
Listen to me and please listen well
When you ride with cocaine you are headed for hell.

Visit Singapore sometime and let me know what you think. I'm open to a second opinion.

The rung of a ladder

was never meant to rest upon,

but only to hold a man's foot long

enough to enable him to put the

other somewhat higher.

— Thomas Huxley

CHAPTER 13

A Round With Betsy King

THE RIGHT *SOUNDS*, like other good things that touch the senses, really are pure joy for us humans. Count among them the click that comes when a golf ball is hit well, when it rises from the tee and screams low and straight into the great fairway beyond.

I have very few regrets in my life, but one of them is that I didn't take up the great game of golf until I was 45 years old. Somehow, I couldn't get excited about stealing five hours from my day trying to hit and chase a hapless ball round a golf course. For my money, and my time, there were better things to do.

In retrospect, it's amazing that it didn't begin earlier. I have lived for many years just five houses from the Vancouver Golf and Country Club, one of the most beautiful and sought-after venues in British Columbia. I pass by its manicured greenery every day of my business life.

But approaching my 45th year, with golf very much in sight, it was completely out of mind. There were other things. I had a speaking career to attend to, a company—Canada Wide Magazines—to build.

But all work and no play was making Peter a rapidly duller boy. My A-type personality was trending toward A plus, I was losing what had been a fairly renowned sense of humour, I had no hobbies other than work and I suspect that the walls of some of my larger arteries were piling on plaque in grand style.

My wife and children, clever females that they are, saw the signs and decided to do something about it. For Christmas that year they got together and gave me everything I needed to begin playing the game of golf—irons, woods, putter, balls, glove, bag, tees, shoes, umbrella. The entire package was under the tree on Christmas morning, and the only thing delaying immediate startup was a turkey dinner and steady rain.

But I did begin and, in my first year, I played 17 rounds, mostly in industry tournaments — the Texas scramble format. It was taking me about 140 strokes to play 18 holes. The second year, I played 75 rounds and I was hooked. Still in industry tournaments, I had also graduated to some of the finer courses around the world. One of the fringe benefits of speaking to corporate conventions is that golf is often on the program, and I am invariably invited to play. It's a real bonus.

I have breathed the desert air on the courses of Palm Springs and Las Vegas, the tropical headiness of Hawaii, any number of others.

In my fifth year, with a score consistently in the high 80's and a handicap of 18, I felt that it was time to move into the big leagues.

John Iacobucci, who is vice president of CKNW

and CFMI, two of Vancouver's most successful radio stations, invited Stan Smith, Vice President, Sales in Canada for RJR MacDonald Inc. and me to be his guests at the du Maurier LPGA, to be held at the Vancouver Golf and Country Club — the one just five houses from my home.

We were entered to play in the pro-am, to be teamed with one of the finest women golfers in the world. As yet, we didn't know who she might be. Tee-off time would be 8:12 a.m.

We were pretty cocky, confident businessmen who had *been* there, *done* that and had *several* T-shirts to prove it. John and Stan were better golfers than I, but collectively we figured a pro-am round would be a piece of cake.

We arrived early on the chosen day, had breakfast at the club, did some putting and driving to warm up for the big round. It was one of those perfect Indian Summer mornings that always remind me why I choose to live in this part of the world, why it's so right to be here at any time of year.

At 8:05, our team was announced over the public address system and in our natty, new outfits we were introduced to the 100 or so spectators.

"Good morning, ladies and gentlemen. Welcome to the 8:12 a.m. tee-off. Playing from the Vancouver Golf and Country Club, with an 18 handicap, the President of Canada Wide Magazines, Mr. Peter Legge!" A courteous round of applause. Then an introduction of Stan, with a 6 handicap, of our host John, with a 15 handicap. We were now on the first tee, with 100-plus spectators, LPGA officials, scorekeepers, caddies and family. We were also starting to sweat. This was big-time stuff, a serious pro-am, and there we were, right in the middle of it.

And our pro? "Ladies and gentlemen, will you please welcome the two-time winner of the U.S. Women's Open, playing out of Phoenix, Arizona . . . Ms. Betsy King!"

Thunderous applause from the gallery. Betsy obviously had a much bigger name than ours. And there was every likelihood that they were respecting the achievements of one of the great golfers of all time.

Betsy walked up and introduced herself. I responded with some rapier wit that somehow came out the wrong way. Betsy looked me right in the eye and asked: "Do you play much golf?" My brilliant brain went into overdrive and came up empty. Stan and John fared about the same.

But it was now 8:12, and with one of the world's best golfers as our fourth, we teed off.

The gods of golf were with us on the first tee and the drives of the three of us went soaring 185 yards right down the middle. Betsy said: "Hey, you guys are pretty good."

"No sweat Betsy, we can carry you this round."

Great start, but for nine holes we ended as complete duffers. Our job, of course, was to be the strong team that supported her round, to give her a chance at the pro-am prize money. On the front nine, it wasn't happening. Betsy spent most of the time helping us pick our clubs, reading the grass of the greens and being a gracious lady.

We pulled it together a bit on the back nine and finished up with a nine under. Respectable, but out of the money.

If you're anything like me, you feel like a beer after five hours of golf. A beer, a sandwich and a review of the game. Would you care to join us? we asked Betsy.

"Yes," she said, "I'd love to have lunch with you except that I have to train for two hours, practice my driving for two hours and work out for two hours."

We shuffled off for a beer, a time to contemplate not just our round, but Betsy's answer, a reflection in very real terms of her dedication to her game.

After five hours of pretty intense golf, Betsy King — already a champion in her field — needed six more hours to finetune her game. We had come face-to-face with commitment. If she were to win future tournaments such as the U.S. Open, she could never let up.

It's true for all of us. Each of us was born with the potential for greatness. Zig Ziglar has said it; many others like him have said it. We were all born to be champions. Maybe not in golf, but champions in the board room, in sales, in some other sport, in art, in literature. We can identify the goal and go for it. Or wander off to the clubhouse.

Commitment brings rewards, *infinite* rewards for those, like Betsy King, who make the commitment to climb to the ladder's highest rung.

In 1992, Betsy broke the all-time record for the lowest four rounds of golf shot by a woman — 68, 66, 67 and 66, a 267 and an LPGA record, set at the Bethesda Country Club.

In 1991, the 55th Masters Golf Tournament was played in Augusta, Georgia. If in that tournament you had shot four rounds of 72, 66, 67 and 72 for a 277 total, you would have won the 1991 Masters, as did Ian

Woosnam from Wales.

If in the same tournament you had finished with rounds of 71, 72, 77 and 71, you would have been right there with Lee Trevino—in 50th spot!

My point is that the difference between first and 50th spot was separated by just 14 strokes over four rounds. (I can drop 14 strokes on one HOLE! I shudder to think of what might happen in four rounds!)

The difference between the ordinary and the extraordinary is really quite small, but the rewards for those at the top are incredible. In the case of the Masters, 14 strokes meant the difference between $243,000 and possibly millions in endorsements for Ian Woosnam, and $3,533 and a chance for Lee Trevino to work his way back and try again.

Being a champion isn't easy, but nothing worthwhile ever IS easy. We are born inheriting the potential to be champions, the seeds are within us. We can seek, find and nurture our talents, and experience the joy and the rewards of helping those talents to grow.

The discovery can come at any time. The lucky ones find it early. For others it takes longer. There is never a wrong time.

I took up the clubs at 45 and found enormous satisfaction in golf. It gave me moments of challenge, but it also gave me hours of blessed relaxation. It also led me to get close to the wisdom and the perseverance of Betsy King. I'm especially grateful for that.

CHAPTER 14

Amazing Mel

I HAVE GREAT ADMIRATION for people who can remember names. I'm not one of them. As I grow older and lose brain cells in the process, I find it becomes increasingly difficult to remember the simplest things — let alone the names of the hundreds of people who come and go in my busy life.

Where did I park my car? What did I do with my keys? WHAT quart of milk? WHO?!

I'm sure that from time to time you've had long conversations with someone you met a week ago and who now is nothing more than a vaguely familiar face.

"So, how did it all work out?"

"Er . . . as well as could be expected."

"No surprises?"

"Er . . . not so far."

And you make an excuse and beat a nervous, frustrated retreat.

I would never deny that it's wonderful to be called

by my name. "Hello again, Mr. Legge, your table is ready." What a great start to a restaurant meal. "Good morning, Mr. Legge, nice to have you with us on British Airways." You just *know* it's going to be a great flight.

There are tricks to remembering names. Some people create rhyming couplets. Lou-blue, Jean-keen and so on. Even better if it matches something memorable, such as looks or personality. Clever maitre d's check reservation books and credit cards to remember names. Others write things down. I think that most of the time this works very well. Nothing like a small cheat sheet as you head out into the cold, cruel world.

Some people, of course, you never forget — and one of them is a man called Mel Cooper.

Mel first inspired me twenty-five years ago, when I worked for him selling time at Radio Station CKNW in New Westminster, British Columbia. Quite unrelated to our continuing long friendship, our BC Business magazine named Mel Entrepreneur of the Year in 1993.

Mel was an amazing guy when I first met him, and as he has matured his achievements and stature have grown exponentially. He now does absolutely everything and has become one of British Columbia's Truly Great People.

These days, Mel is president of Victoria's C-FAX AM radio station and president of two Kelowna, B.C. radio stations, CKOV-AM and CKLZ-FM. He also runs Seacoast Sound, a company that produces music used in ads aired throughout Canada, the U.S., Europe and Japan. He is Chairman of the Board of Air BC and serves on the boards of B.C. Telephone and the Royal Bank of Canada. He teamed up with Jimmy Pattison, another amazing

B.C. entrepreneur, to help rescue EXPO 86 from the brink of disaster. As the person responsible for corporate sponsorships, Mel raised a whopping $174 million to help bring things back on track. Pattison calls him a doer. "When I needed help with EXPO, he was the first and only person who came to mind," said Jimmy.

His EXPO fundraising also made him the first name on the list when Victoria decided to bid for the August 1994 Commonwealth Games. As chairman of the Games' board of governors and chair of the marketing committee, he is confident that the Games' financial targets will be met.

Along with his direct business interests, Mel makes as many as 80 guest-speaking appearances a year throughout North America and serves in honorary positions on the boards of about 30 community groups or charities.

Mark Zuehlke — now *there's* a name to remember — wrote about Mel in our special May, 1993 BC Business edition, and much of this information comes from his excellent profile piece.

What does Mel say about the time he spends away from business? "Even though this might cost me in dollars and cents, I don't view it that way. It's important to me to try to assist people if they think I can help them."

Cooper takes the principle of giving very seriously. It all interrelates with his thinking on realizing dreams. Among his tasks scheduled for a recent Saturday was a meeting with two young entrepreneurs seeking advice on starting their own business. He says he isn't all that interested in helping young people figure out how to finance a new business or develop a business plan. What he wants to do is help them to see a vision of their scheme, help them draw on their own strengths to turn that vision into reality. His eyes light up with genuine excitement when he talks about it.

More quotes that might help you in *your* plans?

"I believe in accountability. People who work for me would say I set high standards. I try to be fair about this. I try not to ask anybody to do anything *I'm* not prepared to do. When I commit to doing something that commitment is a total thing, and I'll go the extra distance to achieve that goal. I'm really motivated by the desire to accomplish a task well. From that I get self satisfaction that makes me feel good."

More? "Nobody rises to low expectations, so always set high expectations and you'll stand a better chance of getting there."

Money? "My focus has never been to accumulate money and I've never considered myself as someone having power. Obviously I want my business to be successful, which results in making money, but that's not the reason I do what I do. What drives me is the sheer love of doing a job well, of pulling dreams together and bringing them to reality. A lot of people have dreams but they don't act on them. I've taken my dreams off paper and made them reality."

Mel — and this is *me* talking again — is one of those people who comes through; when he says he will do something, he'll *more* than do it. Shake his hand, it's a guarantee. Mel Cooper shows up on time, delivers more than you expect, always has one more good idea to put the program over the top.

He's organized. *That* goes *there* and *that* goes *there*.

Mel keeps doing things and the good things in his life keep happening.

I have found that it's always that way. Success and dreams fulfilled come only with hard work. But when you work hard and work well, the success you seek is all but automatic.

When the Commonwealth Games are over in Victoria and the flame goes out in the darkened stadium, we will hear again about how much Mel Cooper's drive meant to the success of that international venture.

And it won't surprise me a bit.

Anyone who adds

to prosperity must

prosper in turn.

— Anonymous

CHAPTER 15

Decorating With Dürer

BUILDING A HOME, whether you're clever enough to do it with your own hands and power tools, or have someone come in to do it *for* you, can really test a marriage. Every step of the way, from finding a neighbourhood that you both like to choosing the colour of the paint on the rec room wall, the task will inspire cruel and unusual decisions and be accompanied by buckets of compromise.

For many of us, it's a foreign field requiring talents we just don't have. Which is why I begrudgingly respect the wages of plumbers, electricians, tile layers and assorted others who do financially well, but also know precisely what they're doing.

A few years ago when Kay and I were in the throes of building our dream home, I came right out with it. Kay, I said, I don't want to do this. I'm all fingers and thumbs and I would prefer to be doing something, *anything,* other than what I'm doing now.

She cleverly sensed that I was speaking from the heart and, to prevent any additional testing of our relationship, agreed to become coordinator of the project. Kay would work with the architect, the principal contractor and all the sub trades and in short order we would have the house of our dreams. I would observe and pick up tabs.

She did a great job. I trotted off to work each day knowing that Kay was up to the challenge. Permits, bricks and mortar, assorted posts, beams, drywall — and paint for the rec room wall — and not too many months later we had ourselves a house.

After the house was complete, Kay continued to demonstrate her organizational skills, her eye for design, by finding all of the furnishings, the bits and pieces of bric-a-brac that would give the house warmth that, along with the family that lived in it, would turn it into a home. That project also succeeded and again I stayed on the sidelines. Kay took a lot of space and really *did* bring it all together, creating cozy corners and welcoming rooms that have been more than comfortable for the Legges and their visitors.

One of the things that Kay bought was a small picture of an owl. (We have many eagles. The owl was a nice change!) I didn't pay much attention to the owl picture for a number of years, knowing only that it was a print of a painting done by the Fifteenth Century German artist Albrecht Dürer, whose watercolours of animals, birds and plants are exceedingly sensitive, whose engravings and woodcuts contributed in a significant way to the German Renaissance.

It was not until I went to the National Speakers

Convention in Orlando, Florida in 1992 that I learned more about Dürer, knowledge that gave me insight and added appreciation for the picture that hangs in our home.

The story was told by my good friend Og Mandino, who writes wonderful books, tells amazing stories and inspires hundreds of thousands of people with his spoken and written words. His most famous book, The Greatest Salesman in the World, was written more than 25 years ago and still sells an incredible 100,000 copies a month world wide. It's available at almost any book store in Canada or the United States, along with many of his others — A Better Way to Live, Mission Success, The Greatest Salesman in the World, Part Two, The Return of the Ragpicker. I urge you to buy and read any or all of them.

Og's story about Albert Dürer opened the Florida conference. Back in the Fifteenth Century, he said, the Dürers, a family of no less than 18, lived in a house outside of the city of Nuremberg. The father worked three jobs just to keep food on the table!

Two of his sons, Albrecht and Albert, were both artistically inclined and both wanted to go to the academy in Nuremberg — but with the army of kids their father had to support, there could be no expectation of financial help for both of them to realize their dreams.

One Sunday morning, they decided to solve their dilemma with the simple toss of a coin. The winner would go to the academy, the other would work in the mines. Part of the loser's earnings would support the other brother and four years later, when the winner graduated, the roles would be reversed.

They agreed to the plan and tossed a coin. Albrecht

went to Nuremberg. Albert became a miner.

Albrecht Dürer was an immediate sensation. His engravings and watercolours were spectacular. In time, his teachers had become his students who marvelled at his work. He began to get commissions, to win adulation throughout Europe.

Four years later, Albrecht returned home and the Dürer family was there to welcome him, to celebrate his accomplishments, his triumphs in the world of art. But most of all, Albrecht came home to toast the four-year sacrifice that had been made by his brother.

Albert, he said, holding his glass high, now it's *your* turn at the academy and *my* turn to take care of *you*. The eyes of the huge Dürer family looked toward their son and brother who now sat with his face in his hands, rocking back and forth, tears in his eyes.

Albert looked up. "It's too late, brother," he said. "In four years, the bones in my hands have been broken by work, the arthritis has crippled my fingers. I can't even hold a glass to return your toast, much less a pen or a brush. It's too late, Albrecht. Too late . . ."

Albert Dürer didn't enter the academy in Nuremberg. But the hands, that were so much a part of the four-year sacrifice he made, were immortalized by his brother. You will know them as Albrecht Dürer's Praying Hands. In supplication, they show the wear of work, reflecting all of the love of that extraordinary relationship.

We don't make it alone in life. Kay's talents helped us to build our home, the sacrifice of Albert Dürer was a catalyst for the emergence of his brother to paint and engrave art for the ages.

We love his owl. It is a face of constant wisdom that

brightens and inspires our lives.

There is a footnote to this story. A speaking assignment in the spring of 1993 took me to Vienna to a conference of key people from the Vancouver firm of H.Y. Louie. Some might say, it's an unusual spot to hold a business conference, but not President and C.E.O. Brandt Louie. His philosophy is to expose his people not only to sights and experiences that are comfortable, but to those that can add new depth and understanding to their lives. With the incredible Louie group, I have travelled to Singapore, Hong Kong and Europe. Next on the list is the Great Wall of China.

But to get back to the point. In Vienna we stayed at the Marriott and it was my intention to use the Albrecht Dürer story as part of my presentation at the conference. None of the Louie people knew that but, soon after we arrived, Brandt asked if I would be interested in visiting the Albertina Graphics Collection, a museum of art in the wing of the Hofburg Palace, behind the State Opera House, opposite the famous Cafe Mozart.

I confess that I really do know very little about art. I suppose that, like many people, I know what I *don't* like. Determining what I *do* like is more difficult.

When I learned that the Albertina not only included the work of Scheidl, Lassnig, Frohner and Disler, but a room full of the work of Dürer, I was ready in a minute.

It was, of course, magnificent and it was all there. I bought a Praying Hands print to make the visit even more memorable and when my turn came to speak, the story of Dürer was told with even more understanding. It was a very special time in an inspiring city.

Imagination is

the key

to motivation.

— René Descartes

CHAPTER 16

And the Cock Crowed

GIVEN THE CHOICE, most public speakers would prefer to speak to large crowds rather than small ones. I always say the bigger the better.

But for others, the thought of speaking to a big crowd turns on the taps of panic and perspiration. Those of us who ache to share our message revel in the absolute rush that a crowd generates, knowing that beyond the podium, the lip of the stage, the curtain that's about to be opened, is an audience bigger than we've ever seen before — thousands of people ready to burst into frenzied, appreciative applause. Give us a dome full of people and we're ecstatic!

Always play to a full house. Better yet, a *big,* full house. Energy pouring back from the most distant, nosebleed seats. How can one *not* be inspiring with an audience like that?

If it's easy and rewarding to speak to a big crowd, it can be quite difficult for us egomaniacs to deliver a message to a *small* crowd. Gather a handful together in a board room, a living room or a community sandlot and we're often less than heroes. Here we're talking to *individuals,* not crowds. The surge of sound, the walls of bodies and faces become individual pairs of eyes, people who can be identified as men and women who are *right there* with the same expectations as those in the stadium or the big hall. But now, you know them — perhaps as Bill and Barb and Ted and Joan. They may be close friends, not strangers who come as part of a larger audience and exit in the night.

There is comfort and energy with a big crowd. These are the gigs we like, the bookings that bring out our best. It's something else again when two or three and not many more are gathered to hear what you might have to say.

About a year ago, with a small group from our suburban Vancouver church, my wife Kay and I went to Israel, a land sacred and important to Jews, Muslims and Christian alike. As Christians, we were making our first pilgrimage to the geography that was the "birthing room" for our Christian faith.

In and around this land are the places where Christ walked and talked. As Mecca is to others, this is where it happened, where the tales of the New Testament come alive.

We flew into Israel from Heathrow with British Airways and ended up in a land that, while functioning like many we know in the West, is full of the anachronisms of another time, the architecture and the social geography of what many of us might recognize as the days of the Bible.

I don't have any doubt at all that there are many

opportunists in places where significant history happened, who have always been quick to take advantage of impressionable pilgrims. There's always a donkey around that's guaranteed to be a direct descendant of one ridden by Christ — and for a couple of shekels you can stand up close and have your picture taken. 'Genuine' pieces of the Cross are likewise available in and around the souvenir shops. They are as plentiful as 'genuine originals' of the American Declaration of Independence, a nice Leonardo da Vinci etching for the den. I find it easy enough to steer clear of all of these things.

But you can't fake the Sea of Galilee, or places like Copernium and Tyberius and Bethlehem. This is home ground for Christians and just to *be* there is stuff for the soul. As I accepted the validity of these places, I also believed in the location of the mountain where Christ had delivered a speech known as the Beatitudes. These Beatitudes are a few incredible verses in the Book of Matthew that give much comfort to those of us who often feel down, downtrodden and generally wretched.

Blessed are the poor in spirit
for theirs is the kingdom of heaven.
Blessed are those who mourn
for they will be comforted.
Blessed are the meek
for they will inherit the earth.
Blessed are those who hunger and thirst for righteousness
for they will be filled.
Blessed are the merciful
for they will be shown mercy.
Blessed are the pure in heart
for they will see God.

Blessed are the peacemakers
     for they will be called sons of God.
Blessed are those who are persecuted because of
     righteousness for theirs is the kingdom of heaven.

"Blessed are the poor in spirit," Christ said, "for theirs is the Kingdom of Heaven." Nice stuff at the start of a bad day, at the start of *any* day.

One day on the tour, knowing me to be a speaker of sorts who generally had something profound to say, I was asked to offer a few inspiring words on the Mount of the Beatitudes when we arrived there the next day.

Would I? Wild horses couldn't stop me! To stand, as a Christian, somewhere in the vicinity of where Christ had spoken some of his wisest, most comforting words, would be a highlight of my life. I was proud, honoured, and humbled.

It was to happen the next morning. I had twenty-four hours to put something together.

As I said earlier, it's a lot easier to talk to a big crowd in a big place. Our group was no more than twenty. The place would be outdoors, in the heat of the countryside of Israel, a long way from Madison Square Garden or any other venue you may wish to name.

Nothing came to me that night and nothing came to me the next morning. I asked myself: Peter, is your mind dead? And the answer came back: Dead blank! Nothing to write down, and twenty people, including my wife, with high expectations from the man with the gift of gab who in just a few hours would be front and centre.

"What are you going to talk about Pete?" Kay asked at breakfast.

"I don't know," I said, "but something will come." I

have always trusted my subconscious to take a task like this in hand. It chugs along while we do other things and quite often, it comes up with solutions. This time, I must admit it was acting with exceptional lethargy.

The bus came later in the morning and we headed out toward "the highlight of my life." It was hot, there were palm trees in the stillness, earth and hills dancing in the humid breezes. Still I had no speech! We got out and stood there, and along with the natural perspiration that came with the day, I prickled with nervousness, sensing that this time Peter Legge the orator, might have nothing to say.

As a prelude to my presentation, Kay asked the group to join her in prayer. I hasten to add that it was not something that was initiated because of my mute predicament. It was a normal segment of a program on a very important morning. With the rest of the group, I bowed my head and closed my eyes.

It was then, along with Kay's words, that I heard a cock crow. Then a second time. And a third.

And Kay said: "Amen." She turned toward me and said: "Today, as we stand together on this mountain of mountains, I call on Peter, my husband, to say a few words. Peter?"

I blinked in the sunshine, thanked her and began to speak. Effortlessly. I told our group how during Kay's prayer, I had heard the cock crow three times. And I said that while it perhaps had no special significance in the state of Israel that morning, there *was* a message in it for me.

Another Peter in another time, I said, had denied Christ in His darkest hour. Peter the 'Rock' had turned away three times when Jesus had needed him most. The New Testament story records the crowing of a cock, a jolting reminder to Peter of his rejection of his friend. Denial in the cold light of personal fear.

I told my group that we all deny our faith, no matter what it may be. Our beliefs become inconvenient or we fear what others might say or do. I accepted the crowing of the cock that morning on the Mount of Beatitudes as a special parable, teaching me not to deny my beliefs. This experience miraculously refreshed my faith. It was very real!

The words had bubbled out, and I felt as much energy from that small group as I have ever felt from speaking to the biggest crowd in the biggest hall. The eyes of some in the group were shining with tears.

Later I discovered that no one in the group but me had heard the cock crow, despite the fact that an active farmyard was just yards from where we all stood.

A modern day miracle? Who can say. But I learned on the mountainside that morning that I must be true, I must not deny.

True to God, true to myself, true to my family, true to my friends.

Though separated by 2,000 years, we Peters have denied our friends, our family, ourselves and our God. But Peter the Rock and Peter the Legge heard the cock crow, wept bitterly with remorse and changed.

CHAPTER 17

Super Silken

VANCOUVER'S EMPIRE STADIUM was torn down in the spring of 1993, something that often happens to old stadiums. With it went a lot of rubble and even more memories.

My father was in that stadium on a hot August 7th day in 1954, when history was made. Along with some 30,000-plus spectators, Dad witnessed the race between England's Roger Bannister and the Australian runner John Landy. For the first time in history, two athletes ran a mile in less than four minutes in the same race. Everest had been conquered the year before and now another "impossible" barrier had come down, another dream of mankind would go into the record books.

Coming into Vancouver for the then British Empire Games, both Bannister and Landy were already sub four-minute milers. Bannister was the world's first, at 3:59.4 in England. Six weeks later in Turku, Finland, Landy did it in 3:58.0.

The world was waiting for a battle of the champions in Vancouver. Who would win? Could Landy beat Bannister?

For many months, Bannister had trained hard in England, setting his sights on a mile in less than four minutes. Regularly, his long-time Oxford friend Chris Chataway paced him, offering him not just challenge, but the inspirational words that might help him change the record books forever.

Despite the "first-person-under-four-minutes" fame that followed his assault on the clock in England, Bannister arrived in Vancouver full of doubt. After attaining the impossible, he now needed a miracle. To win, to beat Landy, must have seemed like a goal beyond comprehension — not helped by many on the sidelines who were saying he could never do it. It *would* be interesting to know, even at this late date, how many of Bannister's family, friends, coaches and athlete peers really believed then that the race and the time might be his. Four times round the brand new Empire Stadium track in less than four minutes — and beat the Australian doing it! The tallest of orders.

For many years, a life-size statue of the record-breaking race's most compelling moment stood outside Empire Stadium. It showed Landy in the lead during the last 150 yards. The drama and the irony was that he was looking over his left shoulder as he ran, the precise moment when Bannister streaked by him on his right and went on to victory. Bannister's time was 3:58.8 and Landy's was 3:59.6. They called it the Miracle Mile.

I have often wondered how Roger Bannister — now SIR Roger, and a teacher at Oxford — kept his dream alive when so many must have fed his mind with the distinct possibility of failure. What an enormous ability to be able to focus so clearly on one magnificent goal.

It's vital for all of us to patiently nurture our dreams. I'm not talking about instant results that can be measured with yardsticks, but Big Dreams. Doggedly driving yourself to achieve the things you want, the things that you have identified as being important to you. In this instant world, where results must happen RIGHT NOW, too many people become discouraged, impatient, depressed, downcast and disheartened. Too many give up too soon. They walk away or run away from their dreams, cop out on life's big opportunities that deliver only when there is persistence, a will to stick with it, to know that records and Landys CAN be licked.

My good friend Og Mandino says: "I will persist until I succeed." And he does, day after day.

Winston Churchill was invited back to his old school to address the graduating class. With great force and a high degree of clarity in his message, the old British bulldog said: "Never, never, never, never, never, never give up." And he sat down to presumably thunderous applause.

We all have an admiration for stickability, for people who succeed because of their persistence. It is so important that we master our own destinies before someTHING or someONE else does it for us.

Henry David Thoreau wrote that if you advance confidently in the direction of your dreams and endeavour to live the life you have imagined, you will meet with success at the most unexpected times. You will put some things behind, you will pass an invisible boundary and new, universal and more liberal laws will begin to establish themselves around and within you; or the old laws will be expanded and interpreted in your favour in a more liberal sense and you will live with the licence of a higher order of beings. How true those words are. I suspect that Roger Bannister had read Thoreau.

Illustration: Rick Thibert

THE MIRACLE MILE
— August 1954

Bannister's big story came in 1954. Some forty years later, another sports story, a different country, the same determination and commitment. This time, a woman.

Many people around the world spent some quality time in the summer of 1992 in front of a television set watching the Olympic Games from Barcelona. On the cover of TV Week magazine in Vancouver, which I publish, we went into the Olympics with a cover shot of a British Columbia rower called Silken Laumann. Coincidence, fate or whatever, she had the potential to be a star. For special reasons, TV Week and the rest of the country was pulling for her.

Training had become a way of life for this 27-year-old and her sights and dreams were clearly set on a medal in Spain. Then in Germany on May 16th, 1992, just months from the start of the Olympics, Silken was injured. She broke her ankle and tore the muscles, tendons and ligaments in her lower right leg. Tragedy! The very engines of her sport had been dealt the cruelest blow.

Give up? Not Silken Laumann. Following the initial shock, she not only began the healing of her muscles, but the stimulation of her mind, to focus again on her original goal — making the Canadian Olympic team, working and winning her way to the medal round, going on. She surrounded herself with positive people who would pump her with the messages that she wanted to hear, stroke the already emerging champion.

She focused not on the hardships, but on the goal. She may well have asked the question: "If not me, then WHO?" "Can I afford to wait another four years for

Atlanta?" Silken had trained and suffered, but inside there was still the will to win, the reserve of strength that had been built up in thousands of hours of rehearsal for this one incredible world moment.

Silken Laumann overcame everything that might have daunted her and won a bronze medal at the Barcelona Olympics. Across Canada, we cheered and cried at the same time. We had been inspired beyond our wildest dreams by the strength and determination of a woman who rose from pain and battled brilliantly to personal victory.

In the closing ceremonies, Silken Laumann carried Canada's flag, the highest honour that can be given an Olympic athlete. When interviewed on television, she was asked what ideals had helped her to overcome her obvious difficulty? What had propelled her to the top, after a tragedy that would have stopped so many of the rest of us?

The Olympic ideals, she said. Silken had kept them front and centre.

Complicated? The best things are never complicated.

Number one: it's hard work. Number two: try. Number three: strive. Number four: be the best you can be.

Never, never, never, never, never, never give up.

Author, motivator and international speaker Denis Wheatley's book Seeds of Greatness addresses the inner strength that lies not only in every athlete but in each of us. And Denis should know; he's been a psychologist for the U.S. Olympic teams for the past twenty years.

Patience, persistence, determination and not only the will to win at all cost, but simply doing the very best you can at your chosen sport or profession, says Denis.

Overcoming the negative input of other people, overcoming the many winds of change and life difficulties that will most certainly come.

Jose Ortega y Gasset said "Human life, by its very nature, has to be dedicated to something."

Each of us MUST have goals and dreams in our professional life, personal life, and spiritual life. We must go after our dreams with the same earnestness, intensity and gusto as Sir Roger Bannister, as John Landy, as Canada's Silken Laumann.

A commitment must be made!

A plan must be laid!

A price must be paid!

— Dr. Robert Schuller

CHAPTER 18

C'mon, Give Us a Smile!

I SUSPECT THAT SOMETIMES IT'S NOT EASY for a flight attendant to stand at the doorway of a 747 and extend a smiling greeting to 400 people who are about to embark on yet another flight to goodness knows where.

Strangers in the day, in the night. Think about what's going on in the minds of all of those people. Some have saved for years to take the vacation of a lifetime, others are heading off to pitch a big deal, others are making a trip of compassion to see a friend or relative who is seriously ill. And on and on. Some are happy, many are stressed out. It's the equivalent of a small town, suddenly being asked to please be seated in a large room, ten seats across — and stay there and behave yourself for the next four, five, eight, ten hours.

And how about the flight attendant? Where is she or he coming from? What happened the night before? How about her or his family? A single mom who's leaving a sick child at home with dad? A guy who has no idea how to handle the problem that came in a phone call just 10 minutes before he left for the airport. And on and on.

But unlike us, the passengers, who stagger down the aisle looking for seat 35A, these people must be at the door — bright, shining, smiling ambassadors of the airline, whose biggest job is to make us feel welcome, prepare us mentally for the journey ahead, to look positively delighted about everything they must do.

As I said earlier, I suspect that sometimes it's not easy for a flight attendant to stand at the doorway of a 747 and extend smiling greetings to 400 people who are about to embark on yet another flight to goodness knows where.

But what value there is in a smile. How calming and welcoming it can be.

Some say that cats and dogs and other domestic and wild creatures get happy from time to time and they too know how to smile. Maybe so, but none come close to the smile of a human being.

"Good MORNING!"

"Here, let me help you with that."

"My, don't you look just spectacular!"

"I'm back, and this time I'm staying."

"Thank you. Thank you SO much."

A smile is our way of doing it, of showing in our eyes, in a unique rearrangement of facial muscles that we feel good about something or someone.

"O.K., everyone, smile!" It sure makes a better picture.

I came across some words that tell it all. The author is unknown, but the words are wise. It's called The Value of a Smile.

It costs nothing, but creates much.
It enriches those who receive,
without impoverishing those who give.
It happens in a flash and the memory
of it sometimes lasts forever.
None are so rich that they can get along
without it and none are so poor but are
richer for its benefits.
It creates happiness in the home, fosters
goodwill in a business and is the
countersign of friends.
It is rest to the weary, daylight to the
discouraged, sunshine to the sad and
nature's best antidote for trouble.
Yet it cannot be bought, borrowed, begged
or stolen, for it is something that is
no earthly good to anybody till it is given away.

You can do it. C'mon, give us a smile!

A man becomes

what he thinks

about all day long.

— Ralph Waldo Emerson

CHAPTER 19

A Penny for Your Thoughts

THERE'S ALWAYS ANOTHER GOOD IDEA around the corner. The big ones don't come often, but they *are* there. The old ones? The old, good ideas get recycled.

In this business, and I'm talking about the broad field of what is commonly referred to as motivation; many of us who are practitioners steal the good ideas. Steal them? Too harsh. Much too harsh. We're recyclers.

We read each other's books, catch each other's presentations, share thoughts at conventions, learn from the perceived shortcomings and strengths of the worst and best in the business.

It's nothing new. Entertainers do it, lawyers do it, politicians do it. Eartha Kitt might say that even educated *fleas* do it. We see someone in a successful niche and if we believe we can benefit by picking up some good pointers, we do — and they become ours. No charge. Thanks very much.

We never regurgitate carbon copies of another person's thought, nuance or idea. We give it our own special kick, hone it, try to make it better.

Is there guilt in all of this? Remorse? Not really. Chances are that as we are making use of something freshly filched, someone is doing the same with something of ours. And someone is always hearing the thought for the first time. It's a win-win deal.

The best ideas and the best books are quoted often. I'm a great quoter of The Bible, not only because I'm a practising Christian, but because I believe that within its sometimes convoluted messages, there is endless wisdom.

Proverbs 12, for instance, says that as a man thinks in his heart, so he is.

Pretty simple stuff, but what an incredible truth. As a man thinks in his heart, so he is.

James Allan, who lived from 1864 to 1912, was a writer who has greatly impacted my life and the lives of many, many others who do what I do for a living. Allan is considered by many to be the front runner for today's motivational speakers, me included. We love his stuff and use it often.

All of us draw liberally from Allan's words and ideas. He identified and wrote about simple things. We respect his brilliance, make use of his material. We believe and have admiration for what he said.

Allan wrote a book called As a Man Thinketh. It was the theme of Proverbs 12 refined for the Twentieth Century. Motivator Earl Nightingale picked up on it and sold more than a million recordings of a presentation he called: "You become what you think about most of the time."

Despite all of this recycling, it's a thought that doesn't go stale. I really believe Proverbs 12, along with Allan, Nightingale and everyone else who has presented any number of variations of that simple thought.

I mention it almost every time I speak. I not only believe it, but I am in awe of its truth. It's like gravity and all those other laws that science has defined for us over the centuries. They are *there*. They *cannot be changed.*

"As he thinks," said Allan, "so he is. As he continues to think, so he remains."

Ask anyone who is "there" or "on the way to being there." They will say that none of us accomplishes much in life if we never dream with a purpose. None of us accomplishes much in life unless we create visions and act to become one with them. Where there is no vision, we perish.

Allan says: "You will always gravitate toward what you secretly most love. Into your hands will be placed the exact results of your own thought; you will receive that which you earn; no more, no less.

"The vision that you glorify in your mind, the ideal that you enthrone in your heart — this you will build your life by, this you will become."

Proverbs said it, Allan said it, Nightingale said it, all of us say it and keep saying it because we know it to be true.

What do *you* think about most of the time? Happiness, wealth, learning a skill, improving yourself, saving for retirement, writing a book, developing a close relationship with your children, being the best employee you can be? None of the above? Some of the above?

Replace or add your own persistent thought and

place this thought foremost in your mind. Write it in your goal book. Visualize having accomplished it. Confront it every morning. (Remember that the first thought of the day directly affects the next twenty!)

As I said, we don't steal ideas in this business. We keep talking about the good ones that have stood the test of time, that are as fresh today as they were when they were conceived.

A penny for your thoughts? What they most often are is what *you* will be. Aim high. Aim very high. And glory in what you will certainly become.

CHAPTER 20

Seal It With a Kiss

When's the last time you wrote a love letter? To your wife? A letter that was important enough for her to tie with a ribbon and keep in a perfumed box forever. The old fashioned kind that oozes adoration, that's full of hearts and flowers.

Things go so fast these days that most of us just don't have time to communicate in ways that people once did. Letters? Who writes letters? A card if you're lucky.

"The presentation went great. See you Thursday. Love to the kids."

O.K., if you don't write letters, let me ask you another question. When was the last time you talked to your wife or significant other in a supportive, loving way? Words that she could tie with a ribbon of imagination and keep in her heart?

You did it when you were courting.

"I don't right know how to tell y' this Betty Lou, but you're the purdiest darn thing I ever saw. Sittin' there on the back of the pickup in the moonlight, swingin' y' legs and smilin' . . . shucks, I ain't never felt like this about a girl every before."

Pure poetry.

And then somewhere along the way, the words dried up.

"Seen m' shirt?"

"What's for dinner?"

"We gotta do somethun' about them darn kids."

The pickup, the moonlight have become a distant bit of history.

The nearest thing to a letter are the words on the birthday card, the flowers sent after the battle of the night before.

"Sorry about what happened." Love?

I have a friend who sends memos to his live-in love. To, From, Date, Subject. You know the kind. He claims that it's a relatively easy way to move the relationship along without a lot of discussion, a precise way to make an important proposal.

"For a long time, we've talked about a new car."

"I've been concerned lately about your weight."

"We had a tough time making love last night and you deserve an explanation."

Occasionally it works, but on many occasions the responses have been spoken ones. Things like: "You've got to be kidding." "You're full of it." "You can't be serious."

But he persists.

I think it's fun now and then to drop a note to your partner. To say something nice in a letter, to mail it.

I got a letter a while back from my wife Kay. It blew

me away, and while I didn't wrap it with a pink ribbon, I have kept it with other things I consider special. Let me share it with you. And no, you may not use it as the letter to *your* love. Your challenge is to write one of your own.

"My Dearest Peter," it began.

I am so thankful to God for giving me a man like you. I don't tell you enough how proud I am of you. Forgive me for that darling. You are so creative, enthusiastic, energetic, strong, powerful. These things are part of you that I love. Somehow I don't convey this. I blunder in when I should be quiet. I should think and see things through your eyes — try to capture a sense of your vision and dream. Forgive me when I have dashed your hopes or crushed your dreams. I will try harder to be sensitive to your needs.

We both know we will never always agree but you are right when you ask me to be a little more sensitive in how I speak and what I say. Continue to help me to learn. I respect your wisdom and honesty and sensitivity in dealing with people, including myself.

I admire and respect the way you love and treat our children. I believe they are secure and confident in themselves because you have treated them with love and respect for their persons. They KNOW they are important because you convey that to them in your loving, caring way.

You have truly provided for us in a wonderful manner. Physically, emotionally and financially. I respect the hard worker in you, the go-getter full of determination and ambition.

I could not ask for more. I have a wonderful, loving, generous husband with a real God-given heart for his family. I thank you for the past sixteen years and look forward to many, many more committed years — till death do we part. I love and admire you very, very much.

All my love forever, Kay.

Wow! I'm certainly no superman, superhusband or superdad, but Kay's letter made me feel like all of them rolled into one. It was humbling. It was a milestone. It was superb.

Write a letter to *your* love. Ask nothing. Offer all. The way you did before.

Seal it with a kiss.

CHAPTER 21

Gird Yourself Well

IN BUSINESS AND IN LIFE, it's important to be up for the challenge, to be prepared for whatever might be coming back at you from the other side.

Henry V of England went to do battle in France with what might have appeared to have been a ragtag, ill-prepared army. But he got to Agincourt and his men sent a hail of arrows forth from their longbows and won the day against the French, made helpless by the weight of their armour. The bowmen are said to have killed between 5,000 and 10,000 and to have taken 1,000 prisoners for the loss of just 13 men-at-arms and 100 foot soldiers.

Did Henry know the power of the longbow? With the imbalance in numbers of troops he was probably nervous in this big "away game," but deep down he must have calculated his strengths.

The story of David's encounter with Goliath is another fine illustration of faith and preparedness, how these two things can work against seemingly insurmountable odds.

I have built a David and Goliath speech and used it in a number of convocations, drawing a parallel between David taking on Goliath and us taking on the world — our careers, jobs, families, problems, inadequacies, fear of failure, relationships, jealousy, health, and any number of other metaphorical Goliaths.

You remember the David and Goliath story. It happened in the Valley of Elah, between the Mediterranean and the holy town of Bethlehem.

David picked up five smooth stones from a stream and tucked them into his pocket. They would be ammunition for his sling against the nine-foot giant Goliath.

But how come five stones when there was only one giant? The scriptures are invariably very specific. One Goliath, it would seem, would need but one stone. Or maybe David figured his chances were slim and he needed a reserve?

The book of Samuel provides the answer. Goliath had four sons, so there were really *five* giants. In David's mind, he needed five stones, one per giant. He was completely up for the job at hand. As prepared as Henry had been for the giants of France.

Do you have some giants in *your* landscape that need slaying. Have you thought about the resources you will need?

Think about your giants as separate individuals, each with a special defence that you need to overcome. Have you identified the giant's weaknesses? Sought his Achilles heel? Discovered a clever way to his soft underbelly?

I may be slinging too many metaphors, but you know what I mean. All I'm saying is that you should never go into anything without being prepared. Those who seek to win, prepare themselves for victory. Before the battle even starts, they have confidence in the way it will end. No surprises.

Be very specific in the armament you choose to take on your giants.

Sometimes a longbow will pierce the toughest armour, a smooth stone aimed well will drop a nine-foot giant.

Gird yourself well. Victory, for those who are prepared, is always sweet.

Whatever the mind of man

can conceive and believe,

it can achieve.

— **Napoleon Hill**

CHAPTER 22

Sowing and Reaping

ALONG WITH MANY OTHERS much wiser than I, I have said often that we are in control of our own destinies.

There are forces out there that sometimes seem as if they might be taking over. But no matter what, it is you who calls the shots on the life you will lead.

Whatsoever a man soweth, that shall he also reap.

Burn your candle at both ends, the day will come when even your middle catches fire.

You may wish as hard as you like when you're buying that lottery ticket, but there is no such thing as luck. Nothing ever happens by chance. Things good or bad that come into your life are there because of unvarying, inescapable law. And it's YOU who's in control of that law.

Consciously or unconsciously it is you who at some time or another produced every condition desirable or undesirable that you find in either your bodily health or your circumstances. You ordered the goods and someday, often when you least expect them, they will be delivered.

As long as you go on thinking wrongly about yourself and about life, the same kind of difficulties will continue to harass you. Every seed must inevitably bring forth after its own kind and *thought is the seed of destiny.*

So how do you steer clear of trouble?

Learn how to think rightly instead of wrongly. By thinking rightly, conditions will begin to improve. In due course, ill-health, poverty and disharmony will disappear. That's the law. You have the power to reverse your unhappy lot, to set yourself on a higher, positive road.

Life need not be a battle. It *can* and *should* be a glorious adventure.

And it's you who will always be the tour guide.

CHAPTER 23

Putting Your World Together

TRY AS WE MAY to work things out for ourselves, it's easy and often very wise to learn good lessons from others. In business, it makes a tremendous lot of sense to look to the leaders for inspiration and ideas. If it's working for them, you say, let's find out *why*.

I have talked to many leaders who tell me that some of their best 'ideas' have been inspired by other leaders. They look to the best and, intentional or not, they transfer the best and make it their own. Thievery? Probably. But many say that everything has happened before in some way or another and we automatically work at ways to share it all. Schmoozing and networking have been around for a long, long time and some of the best ideas have been carried away from rounds of golf, from lunches, from profiles of the rich and famous we've enjoyed in magazines.

It is human nature to seek the most direct route to wherever we're going. This necessity has spawned many an invention. Henry Ford discovered the economies of automobile mass production. The computer came into being because we wanted to *compute* numbers with more alacrity. Freeways evolved because we wanted to take Henry Ford's cars from A to B with greater speed, comfort and safety. Computers have been integrated into both cars and freeways.

I tell a story about a dad who came home late from the office one night to be confronted by his young son who wanted to play. Exhausted, the dad said to himself: "I'll give this kid something that will take him all night, then while he's doing it, I can get some rest."

He had a map of the world that he cut into many pieces, mixed them up and presented them to his son. "When you've put the world together again," he said, "then I promise you we'll play."

Minutes later, the boy came in to delightedly report that he had completed the puzzle. Amazed at the achievement, his father asked him how he had done it.

"On the other side of the world was a picture of a man," said the boy. By putting *him* together, I put the world together!"

Solve the little things, the big things come together. Solve the little things, and you'll be able to spend more time playing with your kids — for the life you dream to live.

No one ever said on his or her deathbed: "I wish I'd spent more time at the office." But they may very well have said: "I wish I'd found a way to live my dreams."

Just off a mythical beach, a swimmer was calling out: "Which way should I go? Which way should I go?" He was 150 feet from the shore and in danger of drowning.

140

The crowd on the beach was unmoved. "Anyway you wish," someone shouted back.

The swimmer went down and when the body was brought to land, it was discovered the man had been blind. It was *direction* he wanted, an audible mark to follow.

How do we know a baby is blind? Because it won't crawl. It has no goal, there's nothing out there to see.

We *live*, in every sense of the word, when we have purpose, when we have small and large goals to follow, when we clear away the imagined obstacles that are guaranteed to block our progress.

If you want to run faster, there's no other way to do it than to train harder. Injury? Of course, the danger is always there but — all things being equal — you will be a faster runner *without* injury.

Others surmount their obstacles and *still* go on to greatness. As a fledgling composer, Beethoven feared deafness, but kept writing his music. When deafness *did* come, he was forced into a world where the only sounds that reached him were those from within him — the remembered music, the orchestras and solo instruments that were still his mind. Beyond deafness, he *heard* the music, projected his very soul onto paper, wrote some of his greatest works. He would never hear them, but they would enrich the world forever.

Success, say the successful, is nothing more than the pursuit of a worthy ideal. It is never attained, because within every successful person is the desire to keep on going. Achieving the *second* million is invariably the product of simply doing the same or more exciting things one more time. The successful people are *driven*.

I read a great article in USAir magazine about the

importance of rehearsal. The story goes like this: when Chinese pianist Liu Chi Kung placed second to Van Cliburn in a 1958 international competition, his career as a virtuoso seemed assured — only to be thwarted a year later when the Chinese government put him in prison for a seven-year term. But even though he never touched a keyboard in jail, he was on tour within months of his release and, according to his critics, playing better than before!

How did he do it without the rigorous, daily practice that's a staple in the lives of world class pianists? Says Kung: "I *did* practice — every day (in prison). I rehearsed every piece I had ever played, note by note, in my mind."

No matter *how* we get there, the most fulfilling lives are those that evolve through planning, that are inspired by goals, that reach out to be fed and refreshed by the best that others have to offer.

I've been told that we may feel like fools for five minutes by asking the wrong question. But by *never* asking a question, we will remain fools forever.

Take risks, stay motivated, be fair in all that you do; make plans, stick to them, go the extra mile, give of yourself as often as you can.

Put your*self* together and in short order you'll put your *world* together.

CHAPTER 24

A Toast to Public Speaking!

IN THE SUMMER OF 1993, I joined a small group of personal heroes who had been similarly honored, by being named recipient of the Toastmasters' Golden Gavel Award at a luncheon in Toronto. Someone in my hometown media called the award the Nobel Prize of International Speaking. Who was I to argue?

Toastmasters promoted the event in its excellent magazine, The Toastmaster. I was flattered to be described as a natural, someone who bonds fast with an audience, who can get people to "laugh, think and cry, all in the same hour."

There's no doubt at all that I love to speak. To be honoured in my craft by a group such as Toastmasters was enough to put me right over the moon!

The big problem, when I first learned that the honour would be mine, was trying to figure out what I would say, how I would present myself when I stood before the Toastmasters audience of 2,500 to be recognized as the best in the business and one of the best in the world.

I settled on a simple theme — they're always the best — the story of David and Goliath, likening those of us who speak to Davids, taking on the Goliaths of industry, the Goliaths of audiences — with metaphoric stones of preparedness. I've written about it elsewhere in this book.

A year ago, my wife Kay and I had been to Israel and had walked the same Valley of Eli where all those years ago David had confronted Goliath, the gigantic leader of the Philistine army. David had rejected an offer of King Saul's weighty armour and sword, choosing instead to arm himself with stones from a brook. A well aimed shot and he could fell the fiercest of giants. We all know that he succeeded.

I came back from Israel with five smooth souvenir stones and I took them with me to the Toastmasters lunch as my armour for the speech I would make in acceptance of the Golden Gavel.

It was a speech about speaking and each stone was a point that I hoped each member of my audience would remember in his or her endeavours.

Point One. **Love speaking so much that you would do it for free.** I have spoken to a lot of audiences, from Fortune 500 companies to children's charities. No matter what the audience, nothing changes. I deliver each message with similar enthusiasm, with the same amount of preparation. Be it 50 or 500, audiences are made up of individuals. Each is entitled to everything you've got.

Point Two. **Prepare, prepare, prepare.** Whether you're talking to a professional association, a community

144

organization or a handful of colleagues, research is essential to the effectiveness of any speech. I often ask for annual reports and mission statements as part of my pre-address research. Each gives me insight into a company's direction, its values and principles. I check the room, the sound system, I check names for accuracy, my notes for the inclusions that will mean so much. Jack Benny, whose timing was impeccable, once said that he rehearsed his ad-libs more than his act. Mark Twain said that he sweated for weeks over "impromptu" speeches.

Point Three. **Speak to those furthest from your message content.** By focusing on the listener who would least understand or relate to the concept of your speech, you are able to encompass everyone in the audience. Put more simply, it means that you don't talk over people's heads. When you are behind a lectern for 45 minutes to an hour, you don't want to lose anyone. There are all kinds of factors you can't control so, if you embrace the whole audience, it's a safeguard. Remember, there's a back row as well as a front row. Aim your message back there, you'll be appreciated all over.

It's not one of my 'stones,' but I do believe jokes that make a point, if told well, can be a most useful speaking tool. A lawyer friend once told me that no matter how serious the subject, a joke is required every 12 minutes in any kind of presentation, whether it's the defence of a serial killer, the delivery of a sermon or a public address. Here's my contribution:

At the Toronto Toastmasters lunch I told a number of story-jokes. One concerned an Englishman's view of heaven and hell that I had seen reproduced on the registration desk of a hotel in London.

Heaven, it said, would be a world in which the police would be British, the chefs French, the mechanics German, the lovers Italian and the organization, Swiss. Hell, on the other hand, would be a world in which the chefs would be British, the police German, the lovers Swiss, the mechanics French and the organization Italian.

I can't quite remember the point I was trying to make, but thankfully there was sustained laughter!

The point was *commitment* for another joke that day. It concerned a husband who showed up at a marriage counsellor's office deeply troubled that the relationship he had once enjoyed with his wife had collapsed, that the spark was gone, that he was ready to leave.

"Give it another chance," said the counsellor. "Break out of the old, tired ways. Do things differently and we'll look at things again in six months."

So the next day the husband bought himself new clothes and new shoes, worked out at the Y, bought champagne and a dozen roses and headed home. Not to the usual back door, but to the front door, where he rang the bell.

His wife came to the door, saw this changed man standing there and burst out: "The kids come home with chicken pox, the washing machine overflows and floods the house, dinner's burnt and now you show up . . . *drunk*!"

Point Four. **Deliver each speech as if it were your last.** One day it might be, and maybe that day is today. As I said in Point One, it doesn't make sense to give anything less than 110 per cent. As with everything in life, do it to the best of your ability. Anything less than a standing ovation is unacceptable.

Point Five. **Tell your own stories.** For years, my presentations were made up too often from the borrowed, begged and stolen material of others. There's no doubt at all that it was wonderful material, but I've learned that my own stories are not only easier to tell, but are more rewarding for my audiences. People are fascinated to hear about personal agony and ecstasy, how the hardships were overcome, how the joy was celebrated. What they say to me later is "if *you* can do it, so can *I*." I feel very good about that.

There is no doubt at all that the Golden Gavel luncheon was one of the most rewarding hours of my life. They just don't come any better than that.

Thank you Toastmasters, and thank you David for your inspiration.

What is, was

What was, is

What will be,

is up to me.

— Unknown

CHAPTER 25

Williams Lake? It's Great!

I HOLD A SPECIAL PLACE in my heart for the Williams Lake Cattlemen's Association. Not because of any particular love for cattle, or for that matter, of any individuals within the association, but because the Williams Lake Cattlemen's Association taught me a very large lesson about life.

In the course of my speaking career, I have jetted in the best of seats to some marvellous international venues. There, in spectacular world destinations, I have been checked into glorious rooms, been served the very best of food and wine, shared conversations with people who have added much to my life experience as they have to the lives of others. To coin an overused bit of language, it's been world class stuff.

Some time ago, I was booked to make a presentation not in Vienna, Lisbon or London, but in Williams Lake, the economic and social centre of British Columbia's fabled Cariboo. This is the home of a boisterous and burgeoning annual stampede, a community where cattle and logging trucks share the highways in a great inland resource empire.

As happens on these speaking trips, things are invariably arranged to minimize stress, to maximize my comfort. If there are not limousines at the airport, there are invariably smiling people who whisk me off in fast, new cars to luxury accommodations. I don't ask for it, but I welcome it when it happens. It's all very bearable.

When I flew to Williams Lake in a smallish plane on a bumpy flight that morning, I was not in the best of moods. Petulant Peter was doing nothing more than going through the motions of an assignment he didn't really want.

At the Williams Lake airport, which is something less than many I've seen in my travels, there was also considerably less than the usual welcoming party.

No limo, just one of those dusty yellow buses that seats about a dozen, the kind you see hanging around every small town in the country. There were no other vehicles.

"I'm expecting a limousine," I said loftily to the driver. "My name is Peter Legge and I'm here to speak to the Williams Lake Cattlemen's Association."

"Hop in," he said, smiling. "This is your limousine."

I really *had* just returned from a speaking engagement in Vienna and — well — was this ever different!

We bumped along into town and my 'limo' landed me safely at the hotel. I was still anything but happy.

It was in the washroom that things changed. There, alone, I looked into the mirror and suddenly and clearly saw the face of a spoiled brat. There in the mirror was someone who for none other than the most selfish of reasons, had stamped a town and an association with values that were his alone, on terms that had *nothing* to do with reality.

What right had I to present myself in a way that was any less than my best? Those people out there have the same kind of expectations as audiences do anywhere. What are you going to do, Mr. Legge? Don't your values dictate that when you stand to speak, you will not only be as good as you were the last time you spoke, but better! Who are you to demand limousines and fancy rooms? These people are as honest, as genuine, as welcoming as any others in your career, maybe even more so?

You're damned right they are, said Peter. I snapped into shape, wiped the dust from my shoes, straightened my tie, combed my hair, added a big smile and went out to knock 'em dead.

I don't think I have ever made a better presentation than I did that day. I *do* remember the standing ovation, the warmth of those people who made their living from the land, who came with high expectations and showed by their smiles and handshakes that they were more than satisfied.

I rode back to the airport in the same bus, with the same driver. Safely stored in the luggage was my attitude, *and* a lesson learned and remembered to this day.

We can never give anything but our best. To do so is to short sell ourselves. This above all: to thine own self be true, said Shakespeare, and it must follow, as the night the day, thou canst not then be false to any man.

Actors give their best when they open off Broadway. They have to. Sculptors take special care with work in the highest, darkest corners of great cathedrals. They know they're doing their work for God alone.

I flew back from Williams Lake that evening with a feeling of exhilaration, of wanting to return to tell those weathered and wonderful cattlemen that they had done me a great favour — because they did. They taught me a lesson and gave me a great story. Go big, or go home!

You never know when something wonderful is going to hit you right between the eyes.

It can happen anywhere. Big places, small places — alone in front of a mirror in a washroom in Williams Lake.

CHAPTER 26

Terry and Rick

NEXT TIME YOU COME TO VANCOUVER, allow yourself some time, some *quality* time, to visit the British Columbia Sports Hall of Fame. It's right downtown, tucked away near the main entrance of the 60,000-seat B.C. Place Stadium, the air-supported bubble that dominates one corner of the city's spectacular skyline.

Visit the hall of fame to reflect on the history of sporting achievement in British Columbia, but spend a lot of your time in the two special galleries that commemorate the monumental achievements of Terry Fox and Rick Hansen.

If you've never heard of them before, your acquiring knowledge of what they did could well change your life.

Terry, who lost a leg to cancer, had a dream of running across Canada. Rick pushed a wheelchair around the world.

Before you even enter the hall of fame, you will see

a monument to Terry outside of the stadium. It's not the most attractive thing in the world, but it's there and Vancouverites and others have probably grown to accept it, not necessarily for its design, but for the person it honours.

"We commemorate the timeless enduring spirit of hope which Terry Fox shared with the world," says the inscription. Terrance Stanley Fox. July 28, 1958 - June 28, 1981.

Terry died of cancer a month before his 23rd birthday.

The miracle of Terry Fox was that he was an ordinary young man who turned his response to pain and loss into a triumph of hope and courage.

When Terry lost his right leg to cancer in 1977, he decided to raise funds for cancer research. He would run across Canada and ask every Canadian to join him in his fight with a donation of $1. He began his Marathon of Hope in Newfoundland on April 12, 1980 with a goal of reaching the Pacific and home which was 5,300 miles away.

As he ran his daily 26 miles, a lone figure with a distinctive hop-and-skip gait, he became a symbol that captured the imagination of the nation. On September 2, Terry was forced to abandon his run when cancer was discovered in his lungs. That morning he had written *3,318 miles* under the date in his diary.

But the Marathon of Hope was not over. Messages of affection and encouragement flooded in and donations to continue the battle against cancer eventually totalled more than $30 million.

In the last year of his brief life Terry received many honours, but Terry Fox will be remembered most as a young man who demonstrated the power of caring, courage and determination and took a nation along with him on his Marathon of Hope.

For his courage and his spirit, Terry was honoured as a Companion of the Order of Canada and the British Columbia Order of the Dogwood, he was Canadian of the Year in both 1980 and 1981, he received the Lou Marsh Award as Canada's Outstanding Athlete, he was named to the Canada Sports Hall of Fame, he was awarded the American Cancer Society Sword of Hope.

Inside the British Columbia Sports Hall of Fame, the Terry Fox Gallery is a collection of memorabilia from this young man's life — a presentation in words, pictures, hardware and electronic images that attempts to show us all who he was and what he did.

The television images roll endlessly in the semi-darkness — Terry running in rain and wind, on lonely stretches of highway, standing tall in a town or city that came out to cheer him on his way.

You read and hear his words. "How many people do something that they really believe in? I wish people would realize that anything is possible. Dreams are made if people try.

"I don't know if it was a dream or a fantasy I had that night. I didn't even know if I'd be able to walk after the operation, but I dreamt that I would run across Canada some day."

In January, 1979, Terry ran his first half mile and by August he was running 12 miles a day. He ran more than 3,000 miles in training and in September, 1979, he decided to begin his Marathon of Hope the following spring. The Canadian Cancer Society agreed to promote the run, sponsors were found and schedules were finalized. Terry planned to run 30 miles a day, seven days a week to reach his goal.

"Being a competitive person, I wanted to try the impossible," he said, "to show it could be done. But most of all I wanted to raise money to find a cure for cancer because somewhere the hurting must stop."

The exhibit includes many extracted entries from his diary, there are T-shirts from the run, T-shirts and letters given and sent to him by admiring children.

A Grade 5 child from Ontario wrote: "You're the bravest person I have known and you're the greatest. Do you know what? I think you are very brave to go across Canada with cancer. I'll never forget the thing you did. I hope you are feeling well."

When he dipped his artificial leg into St. John's harbour to begin his Marathon of Hope on April 12, 1980, few people knew who he was or what he was trying to do. On the highway, the Marathon of Hope was nothing more than a van and a man who hopped as he ran. There was wind and wild weather, there were the hills.

But the miracle had begun. At Port aux Basques, Newfoundland, a crowd of 10,000 pledged $10,000.00. And on it went, gaining momentum into the big cities of Montreal and Toronto where the thousands became the tens and hundreds of thousands. The van and the running man became a new icon for courage and inspiration.

"When I run, I think about the cancer that took my right leg," he wrote. "I think about the people I know who died from it. I think about the suffering others are going through right now. That's what inspires me."

Nearing Thunder Bay, on the western end of Lake

Superior, pain and weakness forced Terry to visit the doctor. "For the last three days I've been feeling a bit nauseous, a bit short of breath." He had pains in his chest and had no idea what they were.

In a press conference at the Port Arthur General Hospital, Canada learned the stunning truth. Terry had suffered a recurrence of cancer and 144 days and 3,339 miles after he had begun, the run would end.

There was no thought that he would die. "I'll do it," said Terry, dreaming of another, better day. "If I can't run, I'll walk, if I can't walk, I'll crawl. If I can't crawl . . . that's somebody else's decision."

A wave of public sympathy grew for this courageous athlete whose quiet determination endeared him to a nation. A surge of donations was followed by a national telethon that raised $10 million, bringing the Marathon of Hope total to more than $24 million — surpassing Terry's dream of raising $1 from every Canadian.

Today the runs continue throughout the world, inspired by Terry's effort. They have raised more than $75 million, giving Canadians and others the opportunity to keep alive the memory and spirit of the Marathon of Hope.

"I'm happy with what I did," he said. "I tried my hardest. I did my very best. If there's any way I can finish it off next year or the year after, I'll be there." It wasn't to happen.

Canadian Prime Minister Pierre Trudeau wrote: "We do not think of him as one who was defeated by misfortune, but as one who inspired us with his example of the triumph of the human spirit over adversity." It was all of that and more.

The Rick Hansen gallery is right next door. Rick's battered wheelchair is mounted on a dramatically lit turntable at the entrance, next to a mural that shows him on the Great Wall of China.

In his great Man in Motion World Tour, Rick wheeled an incredible 40,000-plus kilometres through 34 countries on four continents, returning to a hero's welcome on May 22, 1987, two years, two months and two days after leaving Vancouver.

His marathon raised awareness and created a $23 million legacy for spinal cord research and rehabilitation — and awareness for wheelchair sports. The journey is an amazing reflection of the power of one man's dream.

The Rick Hansen Gallery is dominated by walls of television images, by sounds, by the Man in Motion song that followed and inspired his epic journey.

Again, there are the inspirational words.

One day, he said, wheelchairs will be a thing of the past. Like his own chair, he said, they will find a place only in museums.

"There is nothing you can't do if you set your mind to it," he said. "Have the courage to commit to your dream."

He has praise for the people who supported his effort. "My team has grown a great deal since the day we started . . . they took my dream and made it their own. On my own I couldn't have got this far. As a team we had more ability and strength than we ever thought possible."

Along with the displays of souvenirs from around the world, there are the statistics. Rick wore out 94 pairs of gloves, suffered 126 flat tires and was robbed on four occasions.

He wrote 2,172 postcards, pushed the wheels of his chair 9,000 times a day. He had two birthdays on the road, his 28th and 29th. The best sunrise he remembered was in Toledo in Spain.

His longest day on the road was 16 hours on October 1, 1985. On most days he pushed between 80 and 110 kilometers. They added up at the end to 40,072, or 24,901 miles. He was the recipient of 128 sweatshirts.

Rick had been an outstanding athlete, excelling in a variety of sports. In 1973, at the age of 15, he suffered a spinal cord injury in a traffic accident. His determination to excel didn't stop and even before Man in Motion his efforts as a wheelchair athlete won him wide recognition.

After earning a degree in physical education at the University of British Columbia, he won 19 international wheelchair marathons, including three world championships.

In 1985, after two years of organizing and fund raising, his Man in Motion wheelchair journey around the world began. He would raise funds and simultaneously demonstrate the potential of people with disabilities.

Again the words: "There is nothing you can't do if you set your mind to it. Have the courage to commit to your dream. Reach for the stars. Focus on what you *can* do, not what you *can't* do. Meet adversity head on."

The B.C. Sports Hall of Fame calls these two young men Canadian heroes and indeed they are. "After losing his leg to cancer, Terry Fox was inspired to overcome his disability by his friend, wheelchair athlete Rick Hansen. It was Terry's Marathon of Hope that inspired Rick to his Man in Motion world tour. The achievements of these two outstanding Canadians are an inspiration for our own personal journeys."

The hall of fame is not a place that's often full of people. Most of the time, you'll be there alone. Just you, the sounds and the images in the darkness.

The power of courage will reach out and touch you.

CHAPTER 27

A Little off the Top

SEYMOUR NARROWS is a body of water that lies between Vancouver Island on the West and Quadra Island on the East in the central Pacific coast of British Columbia.

If you've ever taken one of those luxury cruises from Vancouver to Alaska, you will have sailed northward up the narrows, probably at night. The big ships traditionally leave Vancouver at the close of a summer day and by the time you reach Seymour Narrows, it's dark or close to it. The next morning, you will have left the narrows as your journey to Alaska continues — through some of the most spectacular coastal scenery in the world.

Seymour Narrows is half a mile wide. Perhaps it's just as well that the big ships travel at night. Given their size, you're all but touching land to port and to starboard.

Prior to a certain Saturday in April, 1958, you not only would have been close to touching on the sides of your liner, but if it had been low tide or anywhere close to it, you most certainly would have touched bottom, right in the main channel of Seymour Narrows.

In the history of British Columbia, dozens of ships touched bottom in Seymour Narrows and went sliding swiftly into watery graves. But bottom was not the deep of the main channel; bottom was the twin peaks of a devilish piece of undersea geography called Ripple Rock. Most everyone knew that the peaks at low tide were just 10 and 20 feet below the surface of the water. Deep enough to be unseen, close enough to be an exceedingly dangerous marine hazard.

As if that weren't enough to scare the scuppers off the best of mariners, Seymour Narrows presented a second challenge. To the south of the narrows lies Georgia Strait and to the north is the Queen Charlotte Strait, which in turn is backed by all of the water of the North Pacific. When the tide changes, huge amounts of ocean must pass through the half-mile-wide funnel that is Seymour Narrows. Small boats rocked and rolled on carefully calculated tide patterns. Large boats these days surge through at night.

As early as the years of the Second World War creative types tried to figure a way to lessen the fatal toll of the Narrows. Was there a way to remove the tops of Ripple Rock? Others thought a better idea might be to use the rock as a foundation and build a bridge across the narrows to link Vancouver Island and the British Columbia mainland. They went as far as attempting to drill from the surface of the water on slack tides. They could *see* the rock down there. But with predictable regularity, the walls of the Pacific came sweeping in and the idea was abandoned.

In 1953, with more creative thinking, with money, with better equipment and some mighty mounds of explosives at hand, there was promise of a better way to bring the rock down to a more respectable, less dangerous height.

From nearby Maude Island, demolition experts built a shaft downward, then a tunnel across beneath the sea that ended with a shaft upward into the tips of Ripple Rock. And at the end of the five years of work, they stuffed the ascending shaft with more than a thousand tons of high explosives and stood well back. And in April, 1958, they pushed a plunger and the tops of Ripple Rock were blown, along with some very surprised sea life, into history.

There is still a lot of Ripple Rock left down there, but fishermen and fisherwomen and tugboat captains and sailboaters and the captains of luxury cruise ships can now move up and down the important waterway that is Seymour Narrows having to concern themselves no longer with the unseen danger that had always threatened them. The tide still runs as furiously as it ever did, but the top of the rock is gone.

That was a long story, but I tell it to make one important point about life.

Sometimes you don't have to do it all to make something happen for the better.

Of *course* you try for the home run, but the base hit can often be as productive. Of *course* you try for the big job, the big sale, but they don't always come right away. There are often stops along the way that in the end can prove to be enormously important, the stepping stones of

163

fabulous experience.

Try not to be disappointed if sometimes you have to walk before you run. You can't always have it *right now!* Instant gratification may sometimes work for new babies, but as we grow, our maturity is reflected when we begin to realize that battling for our goals is half the fun.

Life, careers, everything happens by degrees. Bit by bit. Most often it's the way we remove our problems, fulfill our dreams, build our savings. Sometimes a *bit* is all that we need to make things a whole lot better.

A couple of hours out of Vancouver when next you're on a cruise to Alaska, you will feel the tide of Seymour Narrows. It will always be there and your vessel will shudder against it or be pushed forward on the flood.

But worry not about the twin peaks of Ripple Rock. Sleep tight in your luxury. The rock, something less than it once was, will slip by beneath you. Silently and harmlessly.

CHAPTER 28

Home is Where the Heart is

For where your treasure is, there will your heart be also.
                                        Matthew 6:21

MY WIFE KAY AND OUR THREE GIRLS have
enjoyed many wonderful holidays together and in recent
years we've been fortunate to have travelled as a family
to some of the most exotic locations in the world.

We've learned a lot about the places we have visited. We've also learned more about ourselves, strengthen-
ing our bonds and charging our batteries in the holiday
process. Why *is* it that we humans often relate better to
each other when we're on vacation than we sometimes
do in our homebound day-to-day lives? I guess that's like
asking why can't it always be Christmas?

Anyway, following the Toastmasters Global
Convention in Toronto in the summer of 1993, we took
advantage of the relative proximity of the locale and
headed off for a break in Bermuda.

It was our first visit to that dot of land way out there in the Atlantic. Sixty years earlier, my father Bernie Legge had been shipwrecked off Bermuda when serving in the British merchant navy. The island's wild reefs came in the way of Dad's 9,000 tonner after it had lost its rudder in mid Atlantic. After ending up on the rocks, Dad and the rest of the crew spent six weeks in Bermuda discovering all of the good bits in and around the island's 21 miles of spectacular length. A tremendous place to recover from a shipwreck!

For *our* trip, Dad as an absent guide extraordinaire had set an itinerary for the rest of us. It was also a blast for him to be able to send us in directions he remembered from an exciting part of his youth.

Despite his earlier unscheduled visit, Dad didn't actually *discover* Bermuda. That honor apparently went to the Spanish mariner Juan de Bermudez, who arrived there in 1503, returning to Europe to tell stories of treacherous reefs, howling winds and strange wildlife. Some say that Shakespeare created The Tempest from those reports, calling the mysterious lands "the still vexed Bermoothes." It may well have been.

My tourist guidebook says that after Bermudez, the island wasn't visited again until almost a century later when in 1593 Englishman Henry May was shipwrecked there. He and his crew stayed just long enough to build a means of escape. What was *wrong* with this man!

On July 28, 1609, also unable to avoid the place on a dark night, Sir George Somers went aground when his vessel the Sea Venture was separated from the fleet sailing from England to Virginia. Sir George, however, was different. Assessing its potential, he viewed the island in a much more positive way and promptly claimed it for England.

Just two years later, a party of settlers began the colonization of Bermuda and I can only guess that soon after, Bermuda shorts and the color pink became the island's new fashion-design statements.

Bermuda is much smaller than I had expected. The only real means of transportation there, other than taxis or the bus, are the motor scooter and the bicycle. We used combinations of all of these modes to visit St. Georges on the far end of the island, the Gates Fort, St. Peter's Church — the oldest Anglican Church site in continuous use in the Western Hemisphere — Featherbed Alley and Confederate Museum, rich with artifacts from Bermuda's history.

St. George's was founded in 1612 and was the original capital. Across a tiny bridge from there is Ordnance Island, site of a replica of the vessel Deliverance, the original of which was built to carry the survivors of the Sea Venture on to Virginia. There is also a statue of Sir George, who you will recall was the first person to appreciate Bermuda's potential as a place for people like us to visit.

I apologize for this long touristy dissertation, but we're now at the interesting part.

Sir George, it appears, fell so much in love with the island that he requested that upon his death, most of his remains should be returned to England but his *heart* should be buried in Bermuda.

Unusual? Somewhat. But here was a man who clearly had found his home, his treasure — and it was, without doubt, Bermuda. In Bermuda his heart would lie, as it does today in a garden on Ordnance Island. England would get the leftovers.

Home, it is said, *is* where the heart is. We are tugged this way and that. We founder in personal ships that plunge rudderless in desperate seas. We crash. We scramble up the rocks. We rebuild and launch again. We find home.

In it, we find the treasures, the goals and aspirations that lie deep in our hearts, the values we set for ourselves. We find contentment.

As I said, a holiday is a wonderful time to assess our personal treasures — family, faith, friends, beliefs, values, community, career.

And perhaps, as Sir George did, to decide where *our* hearts might be buried.

CHAPTER 29

Puppy for Sale – 15 Cents

LARRY LARSEN IS A DYNAMIC SPEAKER and seminar leader. I sat next to him at a National Speakers Association convention in Dallas and we talked.

We discovered early that we had both written books. Books filled with collections of stories and anecdotal material that we have both used in our careers. We recycle the wisdom of two thousand years and add stories of our own. I have said this elsewhere.

In recent times, I have tried to make use of more of my own stories. Many of them are in this book. Others began circulating in my first book, How to Soar With the Eagles.

Larry and I exchanged books. I gave him How to Soar With the Eagles and he gave me his first book, The Winner Within.

The Winner Within tells of the habits of the happy, healthy, wealthy and wise. I have no doubt at all that it will be a bestseller.

In his opening chapter, he quotes football great Vince Lombardi, a man who has inspired so many of us. Winning, said Mr. Lombardi, is not a sometime thing, its an all-the-time thing.

Winning is also an *attitude* — and for so many of us we like winning to be *measurable* so we may move on to the next level of achievement. Remember the question: "How do you eat an elephant?" And the answer? "One bite at a time."

It *is* important to maintain a sense of order in our lives, to break our "elephants" into bite-sized pieces. It's equally important to be able to view the big picture, to get the trees out of the way so we are able to see the forest with a better perspective.

Too many people are majoring in the minors — or to quote yet another metaphor — counting the ants as the elephants go by, getting bogged down with detail when there's a bigger picture to paint.

Larry Larsen's acronym for all of this is SIBKIS, which stands for See It Big, Keep It Simple.

He says he learned the philosophy from a freckle-faced kid who was standing on a street corner near his home trying to sell his puppy.

The kid was dirty, the puppy was dirty, his tiny sign said: "Puppy for Sale — 15 cents."

Larry wanted to stop and help, but he had to keep moving because of a prior commitment. But that night on the way home when the scene was exactly the same, Larry stopped.

"Son, if you want to sell your puppy, take him inside, clean him up, brush him until he shines, put a red ribbon round his neck, get a bigger sign and increase your price."

The boy said thanks and disappeared.

Early next morning on his way to work, Larry saw a presentation transformation. The same boy, the same corner, the same puppy, but WOW! A clean boy, a clean and shiny puppy with a red ribbon round its neck and a huge easel and sign that said: "Puppy for sale - $10,000.00."

Larry thought, wow, this kid is seeing it big all right, but is he keeping it simple? He didn't have time to stop, but two hours later he returned, determined to help the boy get his complete package in order.

To Larry's surprise, the sign was lying on its side with SOLD painted all over it in red.

That's impossible, Larry thought to himself. There's no way that kid could have sold his dog for $10,000.00. He stopped, went up to the boy's house and knocked on the door. The kid came to the door with a big grin.

"Son, did you *really* sell your puppy for $10,000?"

"Yep mister, sure did."

"How on earth did you do it?" asked Larry.

"Simple," said the enterprising young entrepreneur, "I traded him for two $5,000 cats!"

See it big, keep it simple.

Thank you Larry for a great lesson.

We who lived in the concentration camps

can remember the men who walked

through the huts comforting others,

giving away their last piece of bread.

They may have been few in number, but

they offer sufficient proof that

everything can be taken from a

man but one thing:

The last of his freedoms —

to choose one's attitude in

any given set of circumstances

to choose one's own way.

— Victor B. Frank
Man's Search for Meaning

CHAPTER 30

Maggie, the Lady

1986 WAS A GREAT YEAR in Vancouver. It was the year of EXPO, a spectacular six-month-long exposition that attracted some 22 million visits and gave the city new recognition in the world community.

It was also the year that led me a little closer to Margaret Thatcher, a woman I had long admired from a distance as the Prime Minister of Great Britain, who I continue to admire today as Baroness Thatcher of Kesteven, or Margaret, the Lady Thatcher.

We still talk often about EXPO 86. For those of us who were in the city and who came even close to the action, it was like Christmas every day. People came from everywhere and kept telling us how wonderful it all was, how wonderful our city was. You can put up with a lot of that!

Much of the credit for the success of EXPO 86 must go to Vancouver billionaire Jimmy Pattison, a guy who got his own thing going in the used-car business and propelled himself to the business stratosphere in other entrepreneurial fields. He's an inspiring, no-nonsense manager who was exactly the right person to lead EXPO to its widely recognized success.

From the very beginning, I wanted to be part of EXPO, realizing that this could be one of those opportunities that happens very rarely in one's hometown.

My opportunity came through businessman Ray Addington, an incredible personal and corporate mentor, who was the spark behind the British Pavilion at EXPO. Appointed Deputy Director of the pavilion, Ray came looking for associates who would join him to promote the pavilion, its transportation theme and in turn, EXPO overall. I was only too glad to come on board and be part of his team.

We put an ambitious plan together and, courtesy of British Airways, we flew off to Britain to sell our plan to the Foreign Office and other members of the Thatcher government.

Our goal was to raise some $350,000 in cash, which we would finesse into a $1 million advertising and promotion plan that would encourage visitors to the fair and make the British Pavilion the most important stop in their travels.

It all worked, and other than the host Canadian Pavilion, the British Pavilion welcomed more people than any other.

Everyone came, including Prince Charles and Diana, Princess of Wales; Princess Margaret, and, with a Concorde flying overhead, Prime Minister Margaret Thatcher and husband Dennis. It was great stuff, day after exciting day.

174

As I said at the beginning, I have always liked Maggie Thatcher's style and often told Ray Addington of my admiration for this Iron Lady who fought the Falkland War, pushed back the frontiers of socialism, reformed the rules of trade unionism and so much more. In my books she was and is a decisive, no-nonsense, O.K. lady.

I told Ray that Mrs. Thatcher seemed to be exactly the right person for the job in the eleven-plus years she served as P.M. of the land of my birth. I said that perhaps had she been at No. 10 when my father and mother were deciding to leave England for the greener pastures of Canada, they might never have left.

Anyway, Mrs. Thatcher was delighted with the success of the British Pavilion at EXPO 86 and we basked in the warmth of it all.

Five years after EXPO, the Sales and Marketing Executives of Vancouver graciously named me their Sales and Marketing Executive of the Year. There were a number of speakers, old friends and new, who came to shower me with tons of unearned praise. One of them was Ray Addington, who over the years of our relationship has more often than not, surprised me with the unusual. He didn't let me down on that May evening in 1991 at the Four Seasons Hotel award banquet.

Along with his very kind words, Ray pulled from under his coat a personal letter from none other than Mrs. Thatcher Herself, framed most beautifully and ready to hang in my office. She offered congratulations for the award and a thank-you for being part of the success of the British Pavilion at EXPO. I was absolutely blown away.

In 1993, shortly after the release of the first book of her memoirs, The Downing Street Years, Ray arranged for a table for 10 for my company at the Fraser Institute's 20th Anniversary Lunch at the Royal York Hotel in Toronto. Margaret Thatcher was the spectacular guest speaker.

What more could a groupie ask? Ray was and is my hero!

Mrs. Thatcher has said: "The desire to win is born in most of us. The *will* to win is a matter of training. The *manner* of winning is a matter of honour."

She has also said: "You will find it is . . . very lonely being at the top — whether it's the top of your country, your sport, your industry, your profession, your school, your university, your organization. Perhaps one of the loneliest jobs is that of Prime Minister . . . It ought to be: you cannot lead from the crowd."

In her book, Lady Thatcher says that she had the same inner conviction as her 18th-century predecessor William Pitt, the Earl of Chatham, whom she quoted as remarking that "I know that I can save this country and that no one else can."

"He did," she said in an interview in Toronto, "and we did in a way."

How? By having "the principles on which to operate, the policies to which they led and the perseverance to put them into practice." Of these, she said, "it's the perseverance that is the important one."

CHAPTER 31

Starfish, and Other Individuals

NOTWITHSTANDING the recent developments in genetics that, perish the thought, can potentially 'cookie cut' people into clones of themselves, it's nice to know that at this stage of the game no two humans born on this planet since the beginning of time have ever been exactly the same.

You and I and all of the rest of the eleven *billion* have and continue to be unique. I like that. Even more, when I know that we are made in God's image.

Unique though we may be, we *do*, however, have some things in common with the rest of the five billion people who now inhabit the earth. One of them is that we all must live in days that last 24 hours. Too short? Too long? Just right? Maybe none or all of the above.

Suffice it to say that 24 hours is what we all get in a day and much of our success in life depends a great deal on acknowledging the fact that we have finite time to accomplish our goals, dreams and visions. We all have the same allotted number of hours that become days, weeks, months, years and in short order, a lifetime.

When I was in Dallas at the National Speakers Association annual convention, I picked up a copy of The Success Story of America's Most Successful and Dynamic Businesswoman, Mary Kay Ash. You may not have met her or yet bought her products, but I'll bet you have heard of Mary Kay, her team, the pink Cadillacs and all the rest. Remarkable woman!

The book I got was a revised edition of her 1987 best-selling book of the same name. Mary Kay wears very well.

On Page One, she says that there are four kinds of people in this world. They are:

1. Those who *make* things happen
2. Those who *watch* things happen
3. Those who *wonder what happened*
4. Those who *don't know that anything happened*

For most of my adult business life I have been very conscious of time and of the potential value of each day. I have also been very aware of the value of each *person* and of the importance of a single life. Put the thoughts together and apply them, and you become unstoppable.

Michel Eyquem de Montaigne, in one of his sixteenth century essays, wrote: "The value of life lies not in the length of days, but in the use we make of them: a man may live long, yet get little from life. Whether you find satisfaction in life depends not on your tale of years, but on your will."

There are many people — perhaps you are one of them — who find it very difficult to relate to the rest of the world. You believe that no matter what, you don't and can't make a difference. You look around and everyone else appears to be more gifted than you are, more educated than you are, more capable than you are, more prosperous, more connected, more important than you are.

Who am I? you ask. What can I bring to this life? What difference can I really make?

Many people in my audiences around the world seem to think this way. They really do. I get many letters from men and women who are discouraged *even before they begin.* They are convinced that it is their chosen lot to be nothing more than they are, to never make a difference.

Of course, I have empathy for all of you who feel this way and being discouraged from time to time is something that can be very real.

But you *can* change things. Throughout history, there have been so many who have done exactly that, and the world is different and invariably better because of their actions.

Recall the names of Martin Luther King or Winston Churchill or Walt Disney. Recall the dogged determination of grocer's daughter Maggie Thatcher. Recall those in your own circle who decided one day to change, to move on into something better, a higher road.

The power of *one.* The importance of *one.* That's *you,* dear reader. You are that *one,* and all you have to do is believe in yourself.

Edward Everett Hale wrote:

I am only one
But still I am one
I cannot do everything
But still I can do something

And because I cannot do everything
I will not refuse to do the something that I can do.

Be encouraged that through the years, men and women have believed that they are special, that as individuals they *can* make a difference.

- One more vote and Andrew Jackson would have been impeached.
- One more vote in 1645 gave Oliver Cromwell control of England.
- One more vote by a cancer-stricken farmer who rode from New Jersey to Philadelphia in a driving hailstorm to cast a vote, made the United States Declaration of Independence a unanimously supported document.
- One vote in 1875 changed France from a monarchy to a republic.
- One more vote in every precinct in Chicago and John F. Kennedy would not have been president of the United States.

I can hear some of you saying: "Yes, but these were all world-changing events. I'm not even *close* to that stuff!"

Some years ago, an Eastern Airlines jet that was too heavy with ice, crashed shortly after takeoff from National Airport at Washington, D.C. and plunged into the icy Potomac River.

Many died in the crash. Others swam for their lives in the freezing water. In the dark water, it was a scene from a cold hell.

A man named Aaron Williams, driving to make his early shift on time, came across the horrific crash scene, assessed opportunity and dived into the Potomac. He pulled out one passenger, then another, then a third and a fourth, then plunged in again.

Overcome by cold, exhaustion, whatever, Aaron Williams never came back a fifth time. The miracle is that because of what Aaron Williams did on that day, four people lived! *He* died, *their* lives went on.

Where do you place *him* and his individual effort in the scheme of things? I would say without doubt that he's up there with every hero in history. Do you have to *die* to change things? Absolutely not. But change can happen at the edge of a frozen river, it can happen the moment you put this book down.

One morning just before sunrise, an old man walked along the beach and every few steps, he stopped to pick up a starfish and toss it back into the sea.

A young jogger watched him for a while and eventually said: "What in the world are you doing?"

"I'm picking up stranded starfish and returning them to the sea," said the old man. "If I don't, when the sun comes up, they will die."

The young man laughed. "That's ridiculous," he said. "There are thirty miles of beach and a million starfish ahead of you. How can you possibly expect to make a difference?"

The old man took a couple more paces and stooped to pick up yet another sand-covered starfish. With all the strength he could muster, he sent it in an arc toward the rising sun and the cool of the sea.

Then he turned to the young man, smiled and said: "It made a difference to *that* one, didn't it?"

If it has to be, then it's up to me. If not you, then who? If not now, then when?

Others have said: "It is better to light one candle than curse the darkness."

Of *course,* you can make a difference. To your own life, to the lives of others. All you have to do is fix your dreams on your own star, believe in yourself, and *fly!*

CHAPTER 32

Getting from Here to There

- Dr. Robert Schuller

THE GREAT NEW YORK YANKEE baseball catcher Yogi Berra said, "If you don't know where you are going, you'll end up some place else."

So many men and women are completely void of any real goals. They live lives in the main by default.

Zig Ziglar calls them "wandering generalities . . . instead of being meaningful specifics."

Dr. Denis Waitley has observed that, regardless of whether you are an executive in a corporate boardroom or a teacher at a convention, goal setting is more of an art than an exact science. How true that is.

When John Goddard was just 15 years of age, he made a list of all the things he wanted to do in his lifetime. He wrote down 127 goals, among them: write a book, run a 5 minute mile, play Clair de Lune on the piano, read the entire bible, dive in a submarine, sail around the world, explore Australia's Great Barrier Reef, climb Cheop's pyramid, study primitive tribes in the Sudan, explore the Nile and climb Mount Everest, marry and have children.

Were all these dreams foolish and impossible? Not to Goddard.

Today Goddard has become one of the most famous explorers in the world. He has been on countless safaris and expeditions. He was the first man ever to explore the entire length of the Nile and Congo rivers. At last count, Goddard had accomplished 105 of his 127 goals. When asked how he did it he said: "I had a list — a magic list! I wrote the list because I really wanted to do something with my life, I was aware of people around me who got into ruts, had never taken risks, never challenged themselves in any way and I was determined not to go that route."

Goddard was 26 when he arrived at the source of the Nile with his two expedition partners. Government officials told them it was impossible for three men in little sixty pound kayaks to go the whole 4,000-mile length of the river. But their negative predictions only made Goddard more determined. After hippo attacks, bouts with malaria, blinding sandstorms, miles of dangerous rapids and a chase by rifle-shooting river bandits, they finally paddled from the mouth of the Nile into the blue Mediterranean.

"I learned so much about myself on that trip," says Goddard. "About exhilaration of succeeding. It gave me the impetus to go after my other goals. If we had thought ahead to all the miles and problems we'd face, we probably never would have left the tent. But by taking each day at a time we eventually reached our goal. And that's the way to approach life. Most adults equate goals only as business or monetary goals and lose sight of the little daily goals in all aspects of our lives that go to make an entire life."

Many years ago, an old man had lost his way and came across a stranger on the road who turned out to be Socrates. He said to Socrates, "How do I get to the top of Mount Olympus?" And Socrates replied, "Just make every step you take go in that direction."

Brian Tracy says, "The ability to set goals and to make plans for their accomplishment is the master skill of success."

Developing this skill will do more to ensure your success than anything else you could ever do.

Tracy goes on to say that in his twenty-five years of study and experience, he has come to the conclusion that:

Success Equals Goals,
and all else is Commentary

I couldn't agree more. I've also discovered in my own research and study of goal setting that the biggest problem is getting started.

It is goals that help give our lives purpose and meaning.

The very first book I ever read on personal achievement was called How Showmanship Sells by Elmer G. Letterman — published by Harper & Row in 1964. It was a 200-page hard cover book and it sold for $3.95. How times have changed!

Elmer G. Letterman concluded that the one quality that was most predictive of success was what he called "intensity of purpose." That's taking any two people with the same levels of intelligence, background, education and experience. The one with the greatest intensity of purpose will always win out over the other. It's the goals and objectives that you set for yourself that gives you this intensity of purpose.

So many people are looking for different results but just keep doing the same old things.

A farmer prayed to God, "Dear God, please give me a great crop this year and next. I promise to plant some seeds."

Life, farming, business successes just don't work that way.

You do reap what you sow. Cause and effect — action and reaction.

Providing you have clear, specific goals you will be able to accomplish more in the short term than most people accomplish in a lifetime.

I come in contact with hundreds of men and women who have been deceived into believing that the key to success is based upon talent alone or education or brilliance. Some are convinced that being in the right place at the right time, knowing the right people or even waiting for the proverbial ship to come in, will do it.

The great motivational speaker Charlie "Tremendous" Jones says a lot of people are waiting for their ship to come in even though they have never sent it out.

Greatness and success are based on one's determination and persistence in setting and achieving pre-determined goals.

Earl Nightingale described success as "the pursuit of a worthy ideal."

The point is that your limitations are determined

only by your *desire.* How badly do you want to reach your goal after it's set? Only 5 per cent of the population can tell you what they are working toward. The rest are just drifting along.

WHY SET GOALS?

A *Dream* is responsible for every great advance of man. Everything in the world is a dream come true, a goal that was set.

It has been said: "What the mind of man can conceive and *believe,* it can achieve."

It's a skyscraper in Manhattan.

The Concorde. The Euro Tunnel.

A bridge spanning a bay. A corner store.

A home in the suburbs.

A college diploma. A new baby in a mother's arms.

You can compare human beings to ships. Ninety-five per cent of human beings are ships without rudders that drift with every shift of wind and tide. While they have fond hopes of drifting into a rich and successful port, you and I know that for every narrow harbour entrance, there are at least 1,000 miles of rocky coastline.

The chances of them drifting into a port is 1,000 to one. But the 5 per cent who take the time and the discipline to decide on a destination and chart a course, sail straight across the deep oceans of life and reach one port after another.

Ask a ship's captain what his next port of call is and he will answer you in one sentence, one word. Even though he can't see his destination for 99 per cent of his journey.

He knows where he is going and how he's going to get there.

All of us should do the same thing.

Why don't people set goals?

- *Lack of Effort.* It requires effort and hard work to examine life and decide what you want to do. Goal setting requires thinking.
- *Fear of Failure.* It's the most common road block to goal setting.
- *Fear of Success.* Many of us have been brought up to believe it is sinful to desire — let alone to expect to go beyond the normal and blaze our own trail. We strive to be just like everyone else — average.
- *Fear of Accepting Responsibility.* Only people with high self-esteem will set goals. Others say, "whatever will be, will be."
- *Fear of Rigidity.* Goal setting will trap them into a rigid life style. They fear the loss of flexibility. In actual fact, the opposite is true when you focus your energy on specific items.
- *Fear of Change.* If you fear change you won't set goals because you feel setting higher and higher goals will pull you out of your comfort zone.
- *The Right Track Syndrome.* Many people don't take the time to set specific goals. They just tread water and hope the current will carry them to success.

HERE ARE NINE
RULES OF GOAL SETTING

1. Write down your goals.

2. Prioritize your goals.

3. Personalize your goals.

4. Set realistic goals.

5. Get what you need — education, courses.

6. Phrase your goals in positive language.

7. Set deadlines, short and long term.

8. Set goals consistent with your values.

9. Share your visions with those who will hold you accountable. Inspect what you expect.

Harvard Business School did a survey of 1980 graduates and their progress to date. Eighty per cent of the grads had no stated career or business goals. The remaining 20 per cent, who had stated goals and had written them down, were earning three times as much as the group with no goals.

SOME KINDS OF GOALS

1. Spiritual
2. Career
3. Family
4. Mental
5. Social
6. Physical
7. Financial

Perhaps the single most important reason success is achieved by so few is that goals and goal setting are not one of the *habits* we naturally have in our character.

Yes, you can if you believe you can, but setting a goal is clearly the very first step. Where you will be in three, five, ten years from today will be directly related to the goals you set for yourself.

Go get 'em, tiger!

CHAPTER 33

Laws to Live By
- Earl Nightingale

IN EARL NIGHTINGALE'S collection of stories, published some four years after his golden voice was silenced in 1989, he said that our rewards in life will always be in direct proportion to our contribution.

He went on to say that this law is the law that stands as the supporting structure of all economics and of our personal well being.

Unfortunately, most people either don't know about this wonderful rule or think it applies to some other person and not themselves.

The very first line in best selling author Scott Peck's book A Road Less Travelled is that life is difficult. In his follow up book More of a Road Less Travelled, he begins with the words: life is complex.

Historian and Edinburgh-born philosopher David Hume held the view that as men see the world about them, they recognize that certain things always follow other things. This leads them to reason that there is a necessary causal connection between the two things.

Likewise, as men desire something, actions follow which are directed toward securing that something.

For many people, life is a continual balance between fate and our free will.

Hume comes to the conclusion that the universe is characterized by causal necessity, and that there is a relation of cause and effect between a man's desires and the actions in which he engages.

Other great philosophers including Immanual Kant, Descartes, Bacon, Aristotle, and Plato agree with many laws of the universe that will control our lives and the eventual success we seek. And it doesn't make much difference whether we believe these universal laws or not. They are not respecters of persons, they simply work — whether you are young or old, rich or poor, white or black, tall or short, male or female.

Life is difficult and life is complex,
but, it can become easier if you understand the laws.

Ignorance of the Law is no excuse.
– John Selden (1584-1654)

If you have read this far into my book, which is a collection of positive stories and ideas that I hope will have an impact on your life, you are the kind of person who really desires to take control of your own destiny!

If not you, who? And if not now, when? And if not this way, then which way?

In Norman Vincent Peale's book Reaching Your

192

Potential, he says there is a law that like attracts like. If you send out negative thoughts, you activate negative influences in the world through the law of attraction, and you draw back to yourself negative results.

There is no other way it could be. On the other hand, if you send out positive thoughts, bright, resplendent thoughts of faith, you activate positive influences in the world around you, and you draw back to yourself positive results.

Some years ago Canadian author Brian Tracy compiled many of the 'Secrets of the Universe' and recorded them in a best selling album entitled, The Universal Laws of Success and Achievement.

These laws and Brian's album have been one of the most cherished assets of my personal improvement library and have helped me understand some valuable life changing principles that have had a profound impact on all my companies, my speaking career and my precious family.

These laws include The Law of Cause and Effect, The Law of Correspondence — whatever your attitude is, people will reflect it back to you; The Law of Values, The Law of Motivation, The Law of Expectation, The Law of Attraction. The Law of Attraction is considered the granddaddy of them all and has been called the Law of Sowing and Reaping or the Law of Action and Reaction or the Socratic Law named after perhaps the most influential philosopher of all time, Socrates (469-399 B.C.).

Born in Athens, the son of a poor sculptor and a midwife, he lived a life that, while erratic, was one never wanting of more than the simple necessities. He believed in an orderly world, one that had laws that if broken, unlike man's laws, would have a devastating affect on our lives.

Imagine a physicist ignoring Newton's laws or an aeronautical engineer ignoring Bernoulli's laws?

It is essential to learn and understand these Laws of the Universe and use them for good in our own lives.

To begin your pilgrimage you might go and buy a copy of The Sermon on the Mount by Emmet Fox, first published in 1934.

The Law of Life

"Don't criticize
people, and you will
not be criticized. For you will
be judged by the way you criticize
others and the measure you give will be
the measure you receive. Why do you look at
the speck of sawdust in your brother's eye and fail to
notice the plank in your own? How can you say
to your brother, 'Let me get the speck out of
your eye,' when there is a plank in your
own? You fraud! Take the plank out
of your own eye first and then
you can see clearly enough
to remove your brother's
speck of dust."

Matthew 7 Vs 1-5

Emmet Fox says that the words in The Law of Life make up the most staggering document ever presented to mankind.

In these five verses we are told more about the nature of man, the art of living, the secret of happiness, the way out of trouble, the approach to God, the emancipation of the soul and the salvation of the world, than all the philosophers and the theologians put together have told us.

It explains The Great Law. If we were to justify the fanatical saying: "Burn the rest of the books, for it is all in this one," it would be in reference to these words. If we understood for a single moment the meaning of these words and really believed them to be true, we would immediately revolutionize life from top to bottom. Our everyday conduct would be turned inside out. We would be so changed that in a comparatively short space of time, our closest friends would hardly know us.

As we think and speak and act towards others, so will others think and speak and act towards us.

Whatever sort of conduct we give out, we are inevitably bound to get back.

Anything and everything that we do to others will sooner or later be done to us by someone, somewhere.

The good that we do to others we shall receive back in like measure.

The evil that we do to others, in like manner we shall receive it back too.

For every unkind word that you speak to, or about another person, an unkind word will be spoken to or about you.

For every time you cheat, you will be cheated.

For every time you deceive, you will be deceived.

For every lie that you utter, you will be lied to.

Every time that you neglect a duty, or evade a responsibility, or misuse authority over other people - you are doing something for which you will inevitably have to pay by suffering a like injury.

The measure you give will be the measure you receive.

This does not in the least mean that the same people whom we treat well or ill will be the actual ones to return the action.

That almost never happens, but what does happen is that at some other time or place, often far away and long afterwards, someone who knows nothing whatever of the previous action will nevertheless repay it, grain for grain.

If only people realized all this as being literally true, it would have a profound effect and influence on their conduct?

This is a Cosmic Law — The Law of Life.

It is as impersonal and unchanging as the Law of Gravity. It is neither respectful of institutions or people, is never off duty or off guard, is never tired out, is neither compassionate nor vindictive. You can't coax it, bribe it, or intimidate it — and you can't evade it.

Water finds its own level sooner or later and our treatment of others returns at last upon ourselves.

Yes, you can *if* you believe you can. You can grow and develop into a magnificent human being full of life, love and knowledge. Seek and you shall find. Knock and the door will open. The world awaits you.

Soar With the Eagles
with
PETER LEGGE LIVE!

The spirit of this book, its stories, the new and always inspirational ideas of a winner, will add an exciting and powerful dimension to your conference, seminar or sales meeting when Peter Legge is the keynote speaker. For inquiries about engagements, tapes or videos, call Peter at (604) 299-7311 or FAX (604) 299-9188. Or write Peter Legge Management Ltd., 412 Walker Street, Coquitlam, British Columbia, Canada V3K 4E3.

Interested in Communication Skills?

Join a Toastmasters Club in your community. Toastmasters International operate in more than 50 countries around the world.
Write them at:
Toastmasters International
P.O. Box 9052
Mission Viejo, CA 92690-7052
(714) 858-TALK / 858-8255
Fax: (714) 858-1207